Le Guin

DEATH
IN
PARIS
1795–1801

Receipt for '*un Cadavre Masculin*' signed by the *greffier* Bouille at the '*Basse Geol du Cidevant Chatelet*' and dated 8 Ventôse Year VI (26 February 1798)

DEATH
IN
PARIS

The Records of the Basse-Geôle de la Seine
October 1795–September 1801
Vendémiaire Year IV–Fructidor Year IX

RICHARD COBB

OXFORD UNIVERSITY PRESS

OXFORD   NEW YORK   TORONTO   MELBOURNE

Oxford University Press, Walton Street, Oxford OX2 6DP

Oxford London Glasgow New York
Toronto Melbourne Wellington Cape Town
Ibadan Nairobi Dar es Salaam Lusaka
Kuala Lumpur Singapore Jakarta Hong Kong Tokyo
Delhi Bombay Calcutta Madras Karachi

British Library Cataloguing in Publication Data

Cobb, Richard Charles
   Death in Paris.
   1. Violent deaths – France – Paris – History –
   Sources   2. Basse-Geôle de la Seine
   I. Title
   364   HV6970.P/   78–40279
   ISBN 0–19–215843–0

*Printed in Great Britain by
Richard Clay (The Chaucer Press) Ltd
Bungay, Suffolk*

A
mon ami
Jean Vidalenc

Acknowledgement

My thanks are owed to the Ministère des Affaires Etrangères
for assistance enabling the research for this book to be
completed at the Archives de la Seine

Contents

Glossary of Clothing Terms   ix

I. The 'Dossier'   1

II. Beyond the 'Dossier'   29

    i   The *juge de paix* and the historian   31

    ii The calendar of suicide and sudden death:
        emulation and opportunity   43

    iii The *répondants* and the network of neighbourhood,
        work, and leisure   57

    iv The language of clothing and livery   71

    v   Habituation to death   8L

    vi Conclusion   95

Notes   105

Appendices

    1. Records of *4ᵐᵉ arrondissement*, March 1802–June 1803   121

    2. Occupational analysis of the suicides
        and victims of sudden death   124

    3. Addresses established as those of *maisons garnies*   126

    4. Suicides other than by drowning in the Seine   127

Index of Place Names   130

Glossary of Clothing Terms

Basin (or *baƶin*): a type of check
Cannelle: (lit. cinnamon) yellow
Casaquin: a woman's blouse
Casimir: a fine wool (cashmere)
Chine: shot (e.g. *coton chiné*)
Filoƶèle: a rich silk fabric
Futaine: a coarse cotton thread
Indienne: printed calico
Madras: a highly coloured cotton headscarf or square
Merdoye: dark brown
Moucheté: spotted (e.g. *drap moucheté*), in spots
Ramoneur: (in *couleur ramoneur*): jet black
Siamoise rayée: striped cotton material
Toile écrue: unbleached cotton
Turc (*satin turc*): satin in a dark colour

I

THE 'DOSSIER'

'... un silence de cave, de souterrain, un silence qui prenait la valeur d'un avertissement. ... Un bureau, avec des classeurs et une lampe verte, qui découpait, par terre, un grand rond. Un radiateur sur lequel ronronnait une casserole pleine d'eau. Il y avait de la vapeur, de la fumée de tabac et du brouillard. La pièce sentait le mouillé et le désinfectant. L'employé était assis derrière le bureau, sa casquette, timbrée d'un écusson d'argent, repoussée sur la nuque. L'homme, lui, faisait semblant de se chauffer au radiateur. Il portait un pardessus fripé et luisant à hauteur des reins, mais il avait des souliers neufs qui craquaient, quand il remuait. Ils observaient Ravinal qui s'avançait, méfiant. ...'

Boileau-Narcejac, *Les Diaboliques (Celle qui n'était plus)*

'... cadavre masculin ... âgé d'environ 45 ans ... cheveux noirs en queue ... un pantalon de drap moucheté à raies noires, garni de boutons de cuivre jaunes sur lesquels est écrit RÉPUBLIQUE FRANÇAISE, et dessous caleçon de futaine avec les boutons pareils à ceux du pantalon, un bandage autour des reins, dans le gousset de son pantalon a été trouvée une clef de sûreté. ...'

Procès-verbal de la Basse-Geôle de la Seine
en date du 19 germinal an IV

THE BOX D4 U1 7, in the *fonds* of the *justices de paix* of Paris, kept in the Archives de la Seine, entitled *Basse-Geôle de la Seine, procès-verbaux de mort violente (ans III–IX)*, lists the particulars of 404 persons (there are in fact 405 *procès-verbaux*, but one man is listed twice) who met violent deaths through suicide, accidents, murder, and natural causes. The period covered is from 1 Floréal Year III (Monday, 20 April 1795) to 26 Fructidor Year IX (Sunday, 13 September 1801); but there are only scattered minutes for the Year III, a year in which mortality rates reached, for the second year in succession, a record figure of 30,000 for Paris, and in which suicides are said to have been particularly numerous, especially among women of the very poor, so that the documentation can only be taken as fully representative for the period October 1795 to mid-September 1801, a span of six years.

The source does not cover the total figure for sudden death for Paris as a whole during the latter part of the Thermidorian period, the Directory, and the early Consulate. Burials carried out at the expense of the families of the deceased are only rarely included, most of those who come to identify the bodies or their clothing stating that they are unable to pay for interment, so that, in most instances, we are only dealing with the very poor, or at least with those claiming to be so.[1] Suicides, murders, and deaths from accidental or natural causes in areas of the city *other* than the riverside quarters are likewise not included. From the *procès-verbaux* of the *juge de paix* of the *4me arrondissement* for a slightly later period (March 1802–June 1803), however, it seems that most victims of sudden death and suicide had eventually to be sent on to the Basse-Geôle.[2] In fact, about two-thirds of those listed consist of people who drowned themselves in the Seine or were accidentally

---

[1] It is easy to understand why so many close relatives were unwilling to take on the responsibility for the burial of the body of a person who had committed suicide or had been the victim of a street accident, when one considers how much the expenses might amount to, if the decencies due to death were to be fully respected. An elderly man is killed in an accident, rue des Fossés Marcel, Section du Finistère, on 4 Thermidor Year IV. His son and son-in-law declare themselves willing to incur the expenses of a proper burial: 'pour faire transporter le corps mort chez le juge de paix de la Division du Finistaire [*sic*] payé—3 l. pour l'avoir gardé depuis 3 heures jusqu'à 11—2 l. 2s. Pour le transport à Saint-Eustache—12 l. Pour l'ensevelir—1 l. 4. Pour la bière—5 l. Total: numéraire 23 l. 6; pour les frais d'inhumation 30 l. en mandats,' a costly process amounting altogether to 53 livres 6, and *not* in *assignats* (A. D. Seine, D3 U1 7, juge de paix de la Division du Finistère, 11 thermidor an IV, 3me arrondissement).

[2] See Appendix 1, p. 121.

drowned there. This specialisation can be explained in administrative terms, the Basse-Geôle de la Seine, housed on the quayside in part of the old Châtelet, within the jurisdiction of the Division du Muséum (Louvre), on the right bank, being the place to which all bodies were brought, once recovered from the river, at any point between the pont de Charenton and the pont d'Asnières. The Basse-Geôle was the predecessor of the Morgue, established, just after our period, at the eastern tip of the Ile de la Cité.

As drowning was the easiest, and so the commonest, form of suicide, at least in Paris during these years, the documentation can no doubt witness for the general pattern of suicide in the city as a whole, hour by hour, day by day, week by week, season by season, and year by year, even if it cannot be expected to offer a total figure. There were, of course, many other possibilities. But fire-arms had not generally been readily accessible to civilians, save to those in the arms trade itself and to scrap-iron merchants,[1] though they did become, during a period of continuous war ranging from two to eight years, both cheaper and more available, above all on the *quais* in Paris, a city which was not all that far removed from the war zone in 1794 and 1795.[2] By the summer of 1798, the Minister of Justice and the Bureau Central of the Paris police can both be seen expressing fears on the effects of such unprecedented proliferation of *armes-à-feu* and of other murderous weapons, and suggesting means of checking it, by invoking previous regulations aimed at controlling their purchase.[3]

Even so, women were nearly always to prove unwilling to use pistols for the purpose of suicide—there is no single case of them using such a weapon in our documentation—possibly because they were so difficult to use, or possibly on account of some deep-seated natural repugnance

---

[1] '. . . *Jean-François Berleux*, férailleur, décédé depuis 4 jours . . . duquel il appert que led. défunt s'est tué d'un coup de fusil . . .' (procès-verbal en date du 7 germinal an V).

[2] See Note A, p. 105.

[3] A.N. BB 18 758 (Ministre de la Justice, Seine, Ministre au Ministre de la Police générale, 17 messidor an VI): '. . . J'ai trouvé rapporté dans le traité de police de Lamare . . . un édit de Louis XIV . . . du mois de décembre 1666 . . . cet édit me parait suffisant pour vous autoriser à faire arrêter les porteurs, fabricants et vendeurs de ces armes et à les traduire devant les officiers de police judiciaire. . . .' A circular sent out by the Bureau Central on 23 Messidor of the same year also recalls the *ordonnances* of 23 January 1728—the 1720s, in the wake of the long period of wars, having been notorious for every type of physical violence—and of 21 May 1784—in the wake of another war. The legislation referred to applied not only to fire-arms, but to swords, sabres, sword-sticks, and knives and daggers small enough to be hidden in clothing.

for a form of death so dramatically horrible as, in many cases, almost to blow the head to pieces.[1] Equally, swords and sabres, circulating now in vast numbers as a result, first, of the expansion of the National Guard, then of its suppression—it is almost impossible effectively to disarm a citizens' militia—while offering convenient murder weapons, would hardly serve the needs of anyone contemplating suicide; and, even in such military times, a pistol, still an article of luxury, would scarcely be in the range of possessions likely to be available either to the working girl or to an artisan.

For all these reasons, drowning can witness for the general trend of suicide throughout the city. Much the same could be claimed too for accidental death, the river taking a regular toll in bathing accidents, work accidents (the Seine offering not only the principal artery for transport between the east, the centre, and Paris, and between Paris and le Havre, but also containing all manner of floating establishments,[2] ranging from laundry-boats and flour-mills, to public baths, each section of its banks being devoted to ports specialising in the loading and unloading of certain goods), and accidents caused in the process of watering horses, at the various steeply shelving watering-places, *abreuvoirs*,[3] favourite points of masculine sociability, gossip, and exchange of news, comparable to what Eugen Weber has claimed, in the context of the nineteenth-century French village, for the *lavoir*, the

[1] If women proved unwilling to turn fire-arms on themselves, they seem to have shown no reluctance to use sharp weapons on others: Restif describes a murder committed by an aristocratic lady in Paris in the early 1780s: 'tandis qu'il étoit courbé, elle lui plongea entre les deux épaules une grosse aiguille ronde, d'un demi-pied de long, qui sortit par le creux de l'estomac . . .' (*Les Jolies-Femmes*, I). A woman's work-basket could be quite lethal.

[2] '. . . *Marie Gayon*, 21 ans, native de Paris, fille de la veuve Gayon, rue de Sèvres, employée aux bains de Poitevin . . . et qui est tombée par accident dans la rivière . . . en passant d'un bateau dans un autre près lesd. bains Poitevin . . . sans qu'on aye pu lui porter aucun secours . . .' (procès-verbal du 9 thermidor an V).
'. . . *François Rodde*, marinier, 22 ans, natif de Paris, domicilié chez son père, remouleur, 5 rue des Prêtres (Muséum) . . . lequel a eu le malheur de tomber dans la rivière derrière le Pont-Neuf en voulant passer du moulin à farine où il travailloit pour se rendre à terre . . .' (procès-verbal du 26 prairial an V).

[3] '. . . Le C. *Charlemagne Capaumont*, âgé de 15 ans, garçon brasseur, demeurant chez le C. Clerbeau, brasseur, faubourg Denis . . . nous a déclaré que *Jean-Baptiste Capaumont*, son frère, âgé de 20 ans environ, aussi garçon brasseur, même maison, natif de Rusavoine près Noyon . . . étant ensemble à l'abreuvoir dit *le merdeux* et montés chacun sur un cheval appartenant au C. Clerbeau et s'étant trop avancés dans la Seine, son frère . . . a perdu l'équilibre, a disparu . . . lui et le cheval du C. Clerbeau . . .' (procès-verbal du 15 thermidor an VIII).

principal meeting-place for women.[1] To judge from the statistics provided for the Empire by Jean Tulard, the river would have accounted
for from a third to a half of the total of annual suicides.[2]
The *procès-verbaux* are not, however, confined only to the drowned.
They also include those who killed themselves inland, in the area
within the jurisdiction of the *juge de paix* of the Division du Muséum,
those who were murdered, and those who fell down dead from
natural causes and whose burial expenses had to be met by the municipal authorities of the same area. There are also a few instances of
people who died at home and in their beds, but who were buried out of
family funds. For reasons that escape us, a certain number of sudden
deaths and inland suicides from other riverside quarters, on both banks,
are likewise occasionally included in the collection.

In short, the *fonds* would appear to represent the only central
coverage of suicide and sudden death for the whole of Paris, though
scattered evidence has been obtained from the papers of the *juges de
paix* of the twelve *arrondissements*,[3] as well as from the papers of the
commissaires de police of the forty-eight divisions; these last only exist,
and then in incomplete form, for about twenty of the divisions for the
period under consideration (but, when available, we have used detailed material from the Butte-des-Moulins, once again from the
Muséum, from the Arcis, Popincourt, and Panthéon-Français). The
procès-verbaux, despite the limitations that we have outlined, thus offer
a source of considerable interest to the social historian, and especially to
the historian of the very poor and of those just above the subsistence
level, as death among the affluent is only rarely included, when, for
instance, a person of substance from the provinces, whose family is not
in Paris, throws himself into the Seine, or is murdered and his body
then thrown into the Seine.

Of the total of 404 deaths in our principal source, 274 can be clearly
established as suicides (211 men, 63 women); 65 are accidental deaths,
54 of them by drowning; death from natural causes accounts for a
further 56 people; murders for another 9.

Let us first take the 274 suicides. Twenty-five of these were committed inland, away from the river, by shooting, hanging, jumping out
of windows, in the case of a young pupil of the painter David, jumping

---

[1] Eugen Weber, *Peasants into Frenchmen*, Stanford, 1976, and London, 1977.
[2] Jean Tulard, *Nouvelle Histoire de Paris: le Consulat et l'Empire, 1800–1815*,
Paris, 1970, gives a yearly average of 150 suicides, arising to 200 during the
crisis year of 1812. Mercier, *L'An Deux-Mille*, gives 200 for 1769.
[3] See Note B, p. 105.

from one of the towers of Notre-Dame, and, in another, that of a girl, by poisoning. The remaining 249 threw themselves into the river.

The yearly count of suicides is rather more revealing in the revolutionary calendar than in the traditional one, as the most complete run of figures extends from September to September. The totals for the Year III (9) and for Year IV (18) are so fragmentary as to be quite unrepresentative of the gravity of a crisis which, in most towns in northern France, produced suicide rates as high as, or even higher than, those of the Year II (which also witnessed the highest mortality rate for the country as a whole at any time between 1780 and 1817).[1] We can then dismiss them as valueless. The Year V accounts for 29 suicides, there are 44 suicides in the Year VI, 50 in each of the Years VII and VIII, 74 in a little over eleven months of the Year IX.

If we take the suicide count, over this six-year cycle, by revolutionary months, Floréal (April–May) tops the list, with 36, followed by the next month, Prairial (May–June), with 31. The preceding month, Germinal (March–April), stands at 30; there are 26 suicides in Thermidor (July–August); and 25 in both Messidor (June–July) and Ventôse (February–March). Fructidor (August–September) accounts for a further 19, and its peculiar appendage, the *jours complémentaires*, add another 8. There are 20 suicides in Brumaire (October–November), 19 in Pluviôse (January–February), and 15 in the first month of the revolutionary year, Vendémiaire (September–October). The figures drop to 11 in Frimaire (November–December) and to only 9 in the following month, Nivôse (December–January). But there are important discrepancies between the run of figures, over the years, for particular months. For instance, Pluviôse, in the depth of winter, owes its relatively high place in the count to an exceptional grouping of 7 suicides in the Year VI (January–February 1798), whereas Floréal and Prairial maintain high figures for the two Years VIII and IX, and Prairial also for the Year VII. Germinal occupies a high position earlier, in the Years VI and VII; Messidor, Thermidor, and Fructidor all

---

[1] Yves Blayo, 'La mortalité en France de 1740 à 1829', *Population*, November 1975. Between 1791 and 1815, the loss in men as a result of the revolutionary wars amounted to a total of 1,400,000. The worst years before the Revolution were 1741, 1743, and 1747. The annual death rate for the whole of France, Corsica excepted, stood at: 1789—871,100; 1790—865,900; 1791—933,800; 1792—960,850; 1793—879,600; 1794—1,090,300; 1795—824,000; etc. There are once more over a million dead in 1804, nearly a million in 1814. There had been over a million dead in 1747. There were almost a million dead in 1803. The Directory years are if anything a little below average; but the years from 1780 to 1788 all top the 900,000 mark.

attain sudden spurts in the Year IX. Brumaire has relatively high figures in the Year VI and the Year IX. In seasonal terms, the five summer months account for exactly half the total suicides, as against seven autumn and winter months. If, for a moment, we look away from the river, to consider only the 25 suicides committed, in one manner or another, inland, we find that 13 people committed suicide during the five summer months, and that 12 killed themselves during the remaining seven months, and that, of this total, 21 were men, 4, women. Suicide by drowning, among both sexes, seems mainly to have been confined to the spring and summer months, from mid-March to mid-August.

There are, however, significant differences between the sexes. If both strongly favour Floréal (21 men, 15 women), an increasing discrepancy starts with Prairial (23 men, 8 women), though there seems to be an equal predilection for Germinal (18 men, 12 women). Over half (34 out of 63) of the female suicides are confined to the three months Germinal, Floréal, and Prairial; and 59 of these are from drowning. Surprisingly, perhaps, women rarely commit suicide in winter (19 in all, only 2 in Frimaire, 1 in Nivôse, 3 in Pluviôse; but 6 in Ventôse, at the approach to spring), though no doubt the figures would have been very different for the Years II, III, and IV. The Years V to VIII were not ones of exceptional hardship, near-famine, or rigorous conditions of cold.

The suicide count by days reveals a fairly strong preference for Sundays, Mondays, and Fridays (44 each), but Tuesdays still attain 41, and Thursdays, 39. Wednesdays follow with 33, and Saturdays, rather surprisingly, lag behind with only 29. Much more revealing, however, is the daily count by sexes, for, while women show a marked preference for Sunday (15), followed by Wednesday (12), men favour equally Monday and Friday (36 each), followed by Thursday (32), and Tuesday (31). Wednesday comes lowest among men, then Saturday; but Sunday is not particularly favoured. If we were to take all these figures together, it would turn out that the likeliest choice for suicide would be a Sunday, a Monday, or a Friday, in the first half of May.

If we separate the sexes, it is clear that women tended to commit suicide younger, the largest group (18) falling between the ages of 20 and 30, whereas the largest masculine group is that aged between 40 and 50 (54), followed by 30–40-year-olds (there are also a further 15 women in this group). The 20–30-year-olds come low in the masculine count, much lower even than the 50s and 60s, perhaps as a result of economic setbacks, career failures, frustrated ambition, and, more rarely, acute pain and illness (which seem to have accounted for the 16 male suicides aged from 60 to 70). There does indeed seem to have been some sort of correlation, as far as men were concerned, between the decades of maximum expectation (30s to 50s) and maximum disappointment. In this important respect, masculine suicide no doubt presents a far more faithful mirror of the course of public events than would the more private, more intimate pattern of feminine suicide. This would not be to suggest that masculine suicide during these years had a *political* significance, and that female suicide did *not*, but that rather it was more closely related to the general pattern of collective national experience, economic conditions, under-employment, speculation, bankruptcy, the stifling weight of Revolution and Counter-Revolution, the politics of vengeance and fear, war-weariness, the imminence of the next military campaign, and the one after that, the fear of ferocious foreigners, Croats, Hungarians, and Cossacks, even improvements in climate and harvest conditions, such as undoubtedly occurred between the Year V and the Year VIII. So, if there was a notable increase in both masculine and female suicide in the Year VIII, the reasons would probably have to be sought in a private sector that will remain largely impenetrable by the historian, whereas even greater increases in the Year IX may no doubt be related more directly to the general worsening of a public crisis.

While it would be more appropriate to deal in detail with the problem of loneliness when examining individual case histories and when attempting to establish how many *suicidé(e)s* had been living in *hôtels garnis*, it is worth noting, while still on the subject of mainly statistical evidence, that 103 men and 29 women suicides are listed as single, 54 men and 14 women as married, 3 men and 2 women as divorced,[1] and that there were 12 widowers and 11 widows in this melancholy collection.[2] In short, two-thirds of the suicides of both sexes had either always been single or had become so. Suicide among adolescents

---

[1] For instance: '*Marie-Sébastienne André*, épouse divorcée d'Anselme Goubert, limonadier, 1532 rue Saint-Dominique, placée à l'hospice national de Montrouge . . . d'où elle est disparue depuis le 8 ventôse dernier . . . grosses lèvres, le visage grêlé, ayant été brûlée à la joue droite . . . cheveux noirs et gris . . .' (procès-verbal du 15 germinal an V).

[2] There is also one instance in which separation is mentioned in a *procès-verbal*: '. . . *Claude-François Chaboz*, cocher de place, natif de Saint-Gargon près Pontarlier (Doubs), 50 ans, sans domicile fixe, sa veuve déclarant que depuis longtemps elle n'habitoit plus avec lui . . .' (9 floréal an IX).

seems to have been happily rare: 4 men between 16 and 19, and six girls in the same age group.

Loneliness, as we shall see, was in any case strictly relative. Only about 25 suicides are revealed as having no near-relations in the city; and if a half of the suicides seem to have been living in *garnis*,[1] most of them have parents, children, nephews and nieces, and other *proches* giving the same addresses, no doubt often in the same rooms.[2] What is more, 41 of the *suicidés*, 18 of the *suicidées* are native-born Parisians, a further 23 men and 10 women are from the small towns and villages of the *pourtour de Paris*, so that the Paris region alone accounts for 64 men (out of a total of 144 of whom we have the place of birth) and for 28 women (out of a total of 51 about whom we have similar information). Paris and its region thus provide 92 out of a total of 195 suicides of known origin. Thirty-three men and women are from the north-east, 15 from the east, and 13 from the Norman Departments, so that 153 out of 195 are drawn either from the *bassin parisien* or from these provinces. There are 17 southerners (all men), 13 people from the centre, 6 from the west, and 6 foreigners, one of them a woman from Ghent, and men from London, Denmark, Switzerland, and the Rhineland.

In other words, the provincial origins of the suicides reproduce closely the general contemporary make-up of the population of the capital, though the proportion of native-born Parisians (over a quarter, almost a third) is exceptionally high. It suggests that suicide in the Seine was as much part of Parisian *mœurs*, as working beside it, swimming or washing in it, or walking along it. Hence the close, and poignant, relationship between the calendar and the topography of suicide, and those of popular habit, work, and leisure.

---

[1] In the whole list, there is only one person specifically described as a householder: '... C. *Lefevre de l'Isle* (Louis-Jean), 71 ans, vivant de son revenu, veuf, natif d'Aubigny (Cher), demeurant en ses meubles, rue des Bons-Enfants, 1342, Butte des Moulins ...' (procès-verbal du 7 thermidor an IX).

[2] '... enfant mort d'une dissolution putride gangréneuse et que la noirceur de son corps joint à l'odeur qui s'en exhale exigent une prompte inhumation, surtout que le cadavre est dans la même chambre où ils sont 4 personnes dont 2 malades, et que la putréfaction peut augmenter leur maladie' (procès-verbal dressé par l'officier de santé de la Division du Muséum au sujet de la mort de l'enfant de la veuve La Viste, 28 thermidor an V). See also, 'je soussigné officier de santé certifie que la Citoyenne Allemer, décédée, rue de Grenelle No. 68 peut sans inconvénient être enlevée ce soir vu la grande chaleur ... le cadavre ayant déja un degré de putréfaction qui pourroit nuire aux personnes qui habitent le logement ...' (procès-verbal du 8 fructidor an IV).

The social analysis of the suicides of both sexes by occupation[1] is perhaps less revealing of the usual activities of the poorest and least skilled sections of the working population: porters, *commissionnaires*, stable-hands, transport workers and carters, rivermen, *gagne-deniers*, *hommes et filles de confiance*, seamstresses, *repasseuses*, *blanchisseuses*, as well as of those slightly higher up in the social scale, in the specialised and skilled trades, than of the apparent, indeed remarkable, *immutability* of occupation and expectation, from one generation to the next. A dead *gagne-denier* turns out to be both the son and the brother of a *gagne-denier*, while a *regrattier*—an occupation equally wretched and uncertain—has an uncle and a brother-in-law who are *gagne-deniers*. The body of a carter from the north of Paris (faubourg du Nord) is recognised by a nephew and a first cousin who are likewise carters from the north of Paris; another carter, from Clignancourt, is identified by his father, a carter in the same place. A retired laundrywoman is identified by her laundryman son; the body of an *ouvrière-en-papeterie* is given a name by a brother-in-law and a nephew, both describing themselves as *papetiers*. A *garçon imprimeur* is identified by his printer father, for whom he has worked, a carpenter, by his carpenter father, who lives in the same street, a few doors down. The body of a young and—judging from his clothing—dashing *perruquier* is vouched for by his father, a *chapelier*, a trade likewise related to the care and embellishment of the head. Two cousins are *brasseurs*; a *commis marchand de vin*, before his suicide, worked for his *marchand de vin* (elder?) brother; and a *garçon limonadier* did the same for *his* brother, a *marchand limonadier*. A dead *fruitier* is married to a *fruitière*, a dead *journalier*, to a *journalière*, a dead *homme de confiance*, *chez Tapin*, to a cook, also *chez Tapin*. A *marchand de balais* is identified by his two brothers-in-law, exercising the same trade in the same street, but a few doors down (as a character in one of Queneau's novels—*Le Dimanche de la vie*—was to observe, in a twentieth-century context, there would always be an opening in sweeping); a *marchand boucher* who killed himself has two brothers-in-law in the same trade and living like the dead man in Arcueil, a village conveniently placed between the meat market of Sceaux and Paris, though the dead man's niece is described, rather unexpectedly, as *artiste au Théâtre-Français*. A retired *greffier* is recognised by two of his nephews, one a *receveur de l'enregistrement*, the other a printer. Two brothers, one of whom commits suicide, are *carreleurs*, living at the same address, a drowned *doreuse* in her teens

[1] See Appendix 2, 'Occupational analysis of the suicides and victims of sudden death', p. 124.

had lived at her father's, a *doreur*. There is a trio of *grainiers* over the same generation, and a succession of *jardiniers* over two generations.

Signs of an upward mobility, on the other hand, are exceedingly rare in records that give out a repetitive and rather depressing message. A retired *cocher de fiacre*, a wretched trade widely regarded as dishonourable and demeaning, as well as often identified with informing,[1] has an elder son, a 26-year-old *instituteur*, who commits suicide, and a second son apprenticed to a master-printer. A sweeper is seen to have married the sister of another sweeper, no mere *balayeur* however, but an *entrepreneur de balayage*, and is promoted, no doubt as a result of a mildly advantageous marriage, to the post of deputy-sweeper of the Muséum (the Louvre), with a large staff under him employed to sweep the long corridors in that vast palace. An *officier de santé* who drowns himself at the nearest point to the rue de Seine while on leave from the army, has his body recognised by his doctor brother, in practice in the same street. An *ex-employé*, who seems to have gone mad, is identified by his son-in-law, who perhaps has gone up in the world, for he describes himself as a writer in the Ministère de la Marine.

At this level of society, people generally tend to play safe, by using family relationships to consolidate their positions, either in the same trade or in a closely related one. People working in stables are related by marriage; a dead *nourrisseur de bestiaux* has one brother in the same trade and another who is a carter. The brother-in-law of a *flotteur*, accidentally drowned at work, is also a carter; both live in Charenton, which, like Clignancourt, Saint-Ouen, la Chapelle, Montrouge, Vaugirard, and Sèvres, is the natural habitat of those who travel in and out of Paris for their living.

Of course there could also be cases where the unity of the family did not hold, generally no doubt to the disadvantage of its female members. A *rentière*, the divorced wife of a *rentier*, may have felt the pinch before killing herself, while the body of an elderly female inmate of Bicêtre is

---

[1] See my *Reactions to the French Revolution*, London, 1972, p. 79, and Restif, *Les Jolies-Femmes*, VIII: 'Un gros Paysan après avoir été Cocher de Fiacre, en arrivant à Paris [like Guénot] s'était dégoûté de cet état vil, & s'était mis en apprentissage chez un Sellier-Carrossier. Il s'était fait recevoir Maître, & à force de travail, soutenu d'un certain mérite, il était devenu riche dans son état. À l'âge de 35 ans, cet Homme prit du goût pour une jeune, jolie, & délicate personne, fille d'un de ses Confrères....'

Restif then tells a very different story from that spelt out again and again by the *procès-verbaux*. In Restif, people *rise*, hard work is recompensed with success and consideration, only the careless, the foolish, and the very debauched go under. He is concerned with success; our *fonds* with the lack of it.

identified by her former husband, described as a *limonadier*, by her brother-in-law, a *fruitier*, and by her godson, stated to be an *écrivain*. It looks very much as if she had been abandoned by the lot of them, no doubt once she had become incapable of physical work: a case, by no means rare, of the maintenance of the cruel attitudes towards the old and the decrepit displayed by peasant society and transferred to a semi-urban one.[1]

The general impression then is of a very static form of society, its immobility reinforced and perpetuated by family relationships, marriage, common provincial or Parisian origins (even down to the same quarter), and hereditary occupations, and hardly affected, at least once one has reached the Directory, by the circumstances of the Revolution. Most of the occupations listed, especially among the suicides, were in any case so basic, so essential to the continuance of everyday life, as to have been largely unaffected by such exceptional circumstances. No pre-industrial society could dispense with carters and stable-boys, porters, water-carriers, chimney-sweeps, *commissionnaires*, *limonadiers*, *marchands de vin*, *gargotiers*, *logeurs*, *blanchisseuses*, *filles de confiance*, and prostitutes (there is only one member of that profession actually listed,[2] and she is not among the suicides, though temporary prostitution, the fear of disease, the thought of *l'hôpital*, and threats from the police may have driven some of the *suicidées* listed in other occupations to take their own lives).

The actual distribution of *suicidés* and *suicidées* may offer a few hints as to possible economic motivation. For instance, one might expect the largest group to be in clothing, male and female (40), if only because it was such a large section of the working population; but there are sixteen men and one woman (a *rentière*) among the professions, including an *agent de change*, and an *artiste peintre*. If there are twenty-three soldiers, three explanations may be sought for such a large proportion: first, that in any case there would be more and more soldiers about with each successive year of war, and no doubt more and more in Paris, *en rupture de ban*, capitals and very large cities, and their fringes, the inns and

---

[1] On the subject of peasant attitudes to the old of their families a century or so later, see Eugen Weber, *Peasants into Frenchmen*, p. 175.

[2] And she died from natural causes: '. . . a été amenée au poste de la rue Coquillière, sur le brancard, une femme trouvée morte rue de Viarmes, dans l'allée de la maison No. 5 . . . qui d'après l'extrait de naissance trouvé dans ses poches se nomme *Louise-Françoise Garnier*, de Marles en Brie, . . . en date du 19 février 1764. . . . elle parait être morte d'indigestion. Cette femme est reconnue femme publique et sans moyen; elle logeait rue Froidmanteau No 8' (procès-verbal du 6 brumaire an VIII).

lodging-houses of the *faubourgs*, offering the most effective cover to
deserters; that war-weariness would take its mounting toll among unwilling or frightened warriors; and, thirdly, that a number of these
soldiers were in fact veterans, *Invalides* (and one would not have been
there without having been severely maimed: the loss of a limb, of an
eye, or a hand, so as to be incapacitated from manual work), that is
men who, like the inmates of other institutions: Bicêtre, les Petites-
Maisons, may have sought in suicide an escape from constant pain.[1]

The food and drink trades account for only twenty-six suicides,
hardly a significant number; only two are bakers, and they apprentices,
a pretty sure sign that *les années disetteuses* are a thing of the past (or of
the future). There are a few countrymen and countrywomen,[2] and one
or two well-to-do provincials who come to Paris in order to commit
suicide (as to a place where one might choose to do something shameful)
away from the gaze of the family, or who do so as the result of some
fortuitous event—theft, gaming losses—following their arrival there.
In general terms, suicide seems to have owed as much to purely personal
causes as to biting poverty or to sudden economic failure, debt, bankruptcy, or fear for the immediate future. Certainly, the young, well-
dressed former Consul-General in Philadelphia, or the elegant draper
from the family firm in Châteauroux, both of whom we will encounter
later, would seem not to have been subjected to such fears; and one can
certainly discount the pressure of blackmail, very much a nineteenth-
century innovation in criminal specialities.

Perhaps the most surprising absence from this sad catalogue is that
of domestic servants of both sexes, though we do find a few *hommes de*

---

[1] '. . . *Pierre Davit*, paveur, natif de Beauficel (Manche), 49 ans, domicilié à
Paris, 4 rue Chartrière (Panthéon), disparu du grand hospice de l'humanité où
il étoit comme malade depuis quelque tems . . . trouvé noyé . . . en face de la rue
Pavée, quay de la Vallée . . . une chemise marquée *F.* en couleur de rouille qu'on
dit être la marque ordinaire du linge du grand hospice d'humanité . . . le cadavre
est reconnu par Nicolas Turgis, paveur, demeurant place Cambrai, maison de
Saint-Jean-de-Latran, division du Panthéon, et par Julien Faudet, gagne-denier,
demeurant 4 rue Chartrière . . .' (procès-verbal du 3 prairial an VIII).

[2] '. . . *Jean-François Desnos*, cultivateur, natif de Montataire, 44 ans, domicilié à
Mont-l'Evêque (Oise), marié. . . . cadavre reconnu par son frère . . . cultivateur à
Montataire . . .' (procès-verbal du 1er frimaire an VIII).
'. . . *Marie-Félix Rayet*, veuve de Louis Rayet, jardinier à Franciade, native
d'Aubervilliers, 45 ans . . . le cadavre est reconnu par son cousin germain, bou-
langer . . .' (procès-verbal du 29 nivôse an VIII).
'. . . *Louis Denis Breton*, natif de Viroflay, 36 ans, maraîcher, demeurant à
Viroflay . . . cadavre reconnu par ses deux sœurs, maraîchères de Viroflay, et par
deux autres habitants de Viroflay . . .' (procès-verbal du 11 germinal an VIII).

confiance and *filles de confiance*,[1] hybrid beings in that cruelly observant hierarchy, neither quite above-stairs, nor quite below, and often maintained in an enforced celibacy, as 'living in', if they were to keep their positions.

The suicides of both sexes must have pride of place, if only because the time, the place, and the manner of their death were matters of their own choice and the fruits of decisions made individually, even if one cannot discount the persuasive force of emulation, even of habit, especially on native-born Parisians, when it is so often indicated by a whole run of suicides, over a whole week or a month, or by a succession of suicides at the same spot: 35, for instance, in the section of the river running through Passy, 15 underneath, or close to, the pont de Sèvres, 11 off the quayside of the Invalides, 10 off the port de l'Ecole, below the Louvre, 9 off the pont de la Révolution (presumably the old—and the future—pont Royal), 6 off the Pont-Neuf, 5 off the quai d'Orsay, 5 off the port de la Mégisserie, 9 off the various shallow watering-places (*abreuvoirs*).

Even though eighteenth-century topography does not allow for a *pont des suicidés* such as came into general popular recognition a hundred years later with the construction of the romantic parc des Buttes-Chaumont, suicide in the river seems to have had its well-established *hauts-lieux*. Even the *hour* of suicide, when given—generally between nine a.m. and midday or one o'clock—suggests that though the gesture would have been the result of a decision reached alone, probably in the course of a long sleepless night, it also owed something to previous example and may indeed have sought an audience as numerous as possible. In a litany sometimes as repetitive as a suburban time-table, there are only *two* examples of people clearly attempting, on the contrary, to avoid publicity: one, an oldish man, who threw himself in the Seine at four a.m., on a May morning of 1800[2] (even then there was a witness, or perhaps more than one, to record the time), the other a girl who waited till eleven-thirty on a March evening, the same year,[3] before throwing herself in (but she,

---

[1] See Note C, p. 106.

[2] '. . . s'étant suicidé le 8 courant . . . 4 heures du matin dans les bateaux à lessive, arche Marion . . . *François Urbain Léger* . . . 53 ans, ci-devant cuisinier, et depuis ex-militaire vétéran, natif de Soëme-la-Grange près Verdun (Meuse), caserné rue des Victoires Nationales . . .' (procès-verbal en date du 22 prairial an VIII).

[3] '. . . *Marianne Collet*, fille, 28 ans, brodeuse, native de Lunéville (Moselle), demeurante en garnie rue de Viarmes, au *Café de la Paix*, Division de la Halle-au-Bled . . . laquelle s'est volontairement suicidée le 4 du présent . . . 11 heures et ½ du

too, despite her pathetic bid for a discreet death, was witnessed, the hour of her death noted). It seems to have been very difficult to get away with anything at all unnoticed in the constantly observant and close-knit community of this eighteenth-century city, alert even to words murmured in the night and to the muffled sounds of domestic disputes.

The suicides must also be accorded the *place d'honneur* for the simple, but convincing, administrative reason that they formed the principal clientèle of the two bizarrely named *concierges* of the Basse-Geôle de la Seine, Daude (or Baude) and Bouille, the one presumably of Flemish origin, the other displaying unwittingly the face of a clown, a duo in fact that might have been better employed in some comic *rôle à deux* on the stage. Daude and Bouille, however, lived with the corpses of the drowned, spending their working hours among them. It was a peculiar sort of human relationship thus only to have known most of their inmates as dead bodies, though it is just possible that they may indeed have met some of them previously in their lifetime, in this restricted and predictable river world. Anyhow, as a result of their specialisation, they seem to have acquired another, related one: a strange kind of expertise in seams and laundry-marks, darns, leather patches, moles, warts, burns, cottons, silks, satins, corduroys, velvets, fabrics, stuffs, braids, checks, flannels, stripes, nankeens, jewellery, *brandenbourgs*, cuffs and collars, *jabots*, lacework, well-worn shoes, *sabots*, *savates*, even woollen slippers that had walked many streets and even into the beyond, far from Paris. They might have made a secondary line of business as *fripiers*—perhaps they did, though little clothing ever seems to have remained for long in their possession, relatives, who rejected the corpse, eagerly claiming it (and there is one husband, from the nearby rue Saint-André-des-Arts, who, after identifying the body of his wife, missing for the past four days, asks: 'Can I have her ring, her chain, and her broken ear-ring?' which are then given to him[1]

---

soir en se jettant dans la rivière . . . par dessus le quay de l'Ecole, et se tua . . .' (procès-verbal en date du 21 germinal an VIII).

[1] '. . . cadavre féminin, vêtu d'une chemise seulement et nud du reste . . . ayant une boucle d'oreille d'or cassée à l'oreille gauche et point à la droite, et un anneau d'or à la main droite . . . que ce cadavre, la boucle d'oreille et l'anneau d'or ont beaucoup de rapports avec les renseignemens relatifs à l'évasion subite de *la femme Landot* . . . absente de chez elle [rue Saint-André-des-Arts, No 20] depuis 4 jours . . . le mari [imprimeur] déclare que sa femme devoit avoir 2 ou 3 signes bruns à la hanche gauche, ce qui a été vérifié . . . il revient le lendemain réclamer la boucle d'oreille cassée et l'anneau d'or . . .' (procès-verbal en date du 15 prairial an V).

—and their knowledge of medical bandages would no doubt have earned them the admiration of the professors from the other side of the river. Occasionally, in their statements in the presence of the *juge de paix*, they go well beyond their brief, indulging in passages of imagination, putting words in the dead mouths, thoughts in the dead heads: 'She was too tired and too cold,' 'He was sick of life and its infirmities.'

The *suicidés* and *suicidées* represented their special skills; no one in the whole city can have acquired so much information about the appearance of the drowned, no one, not even the police, can have been so quick to spot wounds caused after death (from boat-hooks and so on), and to distinguish them from those caused before it. They even knew what to expect to be the contents of pockets: toys, bits of string, odd objects, in those of a drowned boy;[1] cotton and thread, a tiny piece of soap wrapped up in a handkerchief, in those of a drowned girl;[2] keys, tobacco pouches, snuff-boxes—a standard instrument of sociability, an ideal *entrée en matière* to a hesitant conversation[3]—and pairs of

---

[1] '*Vincent-Michel Chrétien*, natif de Paris, 12 ans, fils mineur dud. Honoré-Simon Chrétien . . . apprenti chez le C. Brûlefer à Montreuil, y demeurant . . . retrouvé à la Rapée, vêtu d'un gillet rond de coutil gris sans manche, un pantalon idem, avec une pièce de cuir sur le genou droit, une chemise neuve de toile jaune marquée *C.H.*, une paire de souliers à cordon, une ceinture de cuir avec une boucle de fer, qu'il avoit dans ses poches un petit clou de cuivre, un petit paquet de fil de cordonnier, un petit bout de ficelle et un petit bouton de cuivre . . . cadavre reconnu par son père, boucher, et par le C. Brûlefer, boucher à Montreuil-sous-Bois, rue du Pré, No 85, étant ce jour à Paris . . .' (procès-verbal en date du 29 thermidor an VII).

[2] '*Louise-Emilie-Charlotte Harmand*, 14 ans, demeurant chez ses parens, 785 rue du Cherche-Midi, disparue depuis le 19 de ce mois . . . cadavre repêché à Sèvres le 22, au lieu dit *l'abreuvoir* . . . une robe de mousseline brodée, un fichu de soye rayé bleu et blanc, un corset de bazin, une chemise de toile blanche marquée *E.H.*, une paire de bas de coton sale marquée *H.*, un petit morceau de savon enveloppé dans un chiffon et une paire de souliers de drap de coton . . .' (procès-verbal en date du 23 messidor an VII).

[3] '. . . Un Laquais mis en sentinelle s'approcha du faux Domestique, & lui frappant sur l'épaule: *Camarade, comment va?—Le geste est trop fort* (répondit froidement Champagne)—*Une prise?* (continua le Laquais, en présentant sa tabatière)—*Veux-tu que je paye la bouteille?—Je ne vous connais pas . . . le trop est trop; nous sommes voisins, & j'ai à te parler de choses importantes . . .*' The snuff-box eventually does the trick, and the young man is engaged in conversation (Restif, *Les Parisiennes*, IV).

The contents of the pockets of a *suicidée*, the wife of a captain in the *armée d'Italie*, include 'une tabatière en coffret de composition ovale, un couteau à manche d'ivoire, cassé, garni de sa lame, et d'un tire-bouchon et un petit étui en bois d'ébène . . .' (procès-verbal du 23 prairial an V).   (See footnote continued over.)

spectacles, in those of drowned adults (of either sex);[1] identity cards, left intact, to guide them, or torn up, to make things more difficult for them.

But they also had to take in whatever else was brought to them, at least from within the Division du Muséum: old people who had fallen down dead in the street, the bloody remains of those who had shot themselves, those who had thrown themselves out of windows, men and women who had hanged themselves, even two women, or what was left of them, who had been blown to pieces by the explosion of the Infernal Machine of the rue Nicaise, and, above all, the victims, many of them children, of accidental drowning.

In this group of 65 people who had accidentally died, 54 had been drowned, 8 more had been killed in work accidents, one woman had been run over by a cab, and there were the two victims of the bomb meant to kill Bonaparte. Of the 54 accidentally drowned, 25 were boys ranging in age from 7 to 17, 5 of them aged 13, another 5 aged 14; all were drowned while bathing. Two more were girls of 10 and 11, one drowned while washing clothes in the river, the other having been sent to fill a pail of water on steps leading down to the level of the Seine (*escalier des Grands Degrés*). Another 17 were young men, 2 were girls aged 21 and 22 sufficiently daring to have followed the example of the young male swimmers.

The calendar of accidental drowning presents few surprises and no problems: 5 in June, 11 in July, 22 in August, 15 on a Monday, 10 on a Friday, 8 on a Sunday.[2] There is a veritable run of such drownings in two successive summers: 6, 7, 15 July, 1, 8, 11, 12 August 1799; 4, 9 (twice) July, 1, 2, 3 (twice), 4, 5, 14, 17, 18, 21, and 26 August 1800, from which it might be inferred that each was very hot. Most such accidental drownings are described as occurring between six in the

---

(*cont.*) Paulmier de Chamarande, aged 70, died suddenly in the street, Cloître Saint-Honoré. His pockets contained 'un mouchoir, une paire de gants de peau, une petite brosse, une tabatière de carton, un petit *almanack* surlequel est écrit *l'année Onzieme* . . .' (28 ventôse an XI, D4 U1 31).

[1] A 55-year-old Parisian is recovered drowned from the river wearing 'une mauvaise chemise de femme sans marque . . .', and in his pockets, 'un petit porte-feuille de maroquin rouge dans lequel étoit renfermée une paire de lunettes . . .'.

[2] Swimming, too, was a form of popular sociability, enabling people to meet one another. People went to the river in groups of twos and threes. Opdeweert, a 14-year-old Belgian apprentice, is drowned, port Nicolas, the same day as a certain Villetard, aged 36 and from the Somme. They were presumably drowned together, 14 Thermidor Year VIII.

evening and midnight, that is at the opposite end of the day to suicides.[1]
But young men drowned after being dragged into the river by their
horses, while attempting to water them, disappear with one or several
of their mounts early on Sunday or Monday morning. Rivermen, who
were no more likely to be able to swim than anyone else, and girls
working on laundry-boats or on floating bathing establishments, might
be drowned any working day of the week.

The calendar of death from natural causes is unrewarding. People
are said to have died of cold in December, one is said to have died of
cold on 16 July (1799). Most such deaths are ascribed, in summer, to
apoplexy, blood pressure, and so on, in winter to lung failure, *suffo-
quement, indigestion*; half a dozen old people enjoy the relative luxury of
being able to die alone, one, a retired *marchand de têtes de veau*, only
being found, in an advanced state of decomposition, a little more than
a skeleton, with all his fat dried up, after three months;[2] more often,
their bodies are hastily removed from rooms in which several other
people are living. One or two obligingly die in company, while on a
visit, one to a *notaire*,[3] or at the end of a meal in a *gargote*, the happy fate
of a pauper of nearly eighty-one,[4] as well as of a cab-driver who had left
his cab at an authorised rank to go and eat a *pot-au-feu*, and who, despite

---

[1] For instance, 'noyé le 16 à 11 heures du soir, en se baignant devant le Champ de
Mars *Etienne-Firmin Lefebvre*, 23 ans, natif de Capit [Cappy] (Somme), élève en chi-
rurgie, demeurant hospice de l'Unité . . .' (procès-verbal du 17 thermidor an VIII).

[2] '*Jacques Mique* . . . marchand de têtes de veau, mort de mort subite . . . étant
mort suivant les apparances depuis plus de trois mois, la graisse et les chairs
toutes desséchées et le (—?) des os et la putréfaction étant telle qu'elle se fait
sentir dans toute la maison (—?) rue des Marchés . . .' (procès-verbal en date du
7 vendémiaire an V).

[3] '. . . *Delahaye*, rentier, 121 rue Croix-des-Petits-Champs, mort subitement
chez Glaizot, homme de loi, 21 rue Guénégaud sur les 7 heures du soir, client
dud. Glaizot chez lequel il s'étoit rendu pour lui parler de ses affaires, par une
attaque d'apoléxie qui peut lui avoir été occasionnée par le froid . . .' (procès-
verbal du 28 messidor an VII).

[4] 'Appert que le cadavre masculin décédé subitement dans un cabaret, rue de la
Grande Truanderie No 15, chez le C. Girardot, marchand de vin, absent de son
domicile le 12 prairial . . . est bien celui du C. *Jean Duval*, cordonnier, natif de
Paris . . . près de 81 ans, demeurant Maison Nationale dite des Petites Maisons, rue
de la Chaise No 525, Division de l'Ouest, led. Duval veuf . . .' (procès-verbal du
16 prairial an IX).

See also: '*Claude Brun*, garçon tailleur, 53 ans, natif de Méximieux (Ain),
demeurant à Paris, rue de la Chanvrerie . . . décédé subitement chez le C. Herbil-
lon, traiteur, rue du Crucifix . . . n'a d'autre objet qu'une cause naturelle . . . un
vieux gilet, une vieille culotte de satin . . . une paire de gros souliers avec boucles
de cuivre . . . une chemise, un chapeau à trois cornes . . .' (procès-verbal du 30
vendémiaire an VII).

all inquiries, escaped identification.[1] An elderly pensioner fell down dead
while walking in a vineyard in Clamart on a Sunday afternoon.[2] Most
seem indeed to have justified the title on the box: *mort violente*, being
suddenly overtaken by death without warning, one of them falling
downstairs at midnight, on the way to his cellar[3] (he did not reach his
wine, whereas the 80-year-old inmate of Bicêtre who had died in a
gargote, had emptied a two-pint bottle, and finished a meal—the combination may even have killed him—with, as it turned out, only a few
liards and an old key and a broken corkscrew in his pocket). But we
hear of one woman sitting on a stool and vomiting blood into an
earthenware pot in front of her, till she fell over backwards, blocking
the door with her body;[4] she was one of the unlucky ones, death not
taking her completely by surprise. As most were very poor, it was perhaps just as well that death should have come upon them so fast,
rather than lingering at their bedside, for most had no one to look
after them and would not have been able to afford long periods in bed,
even assuming that they actually had the use of a bed in the daytime; if
they were in a *garni*, they would have to relinquish the bed to a night-
worker, early in the morning. Certainly when they did die, they had
little to take with them or leave behind them, little more than the
clothes that they died in; of the room vacated as the result of sudden
death by a 66-year-old *gagne-denier*, the *juge de paix* notes: 'dans ce
cabinet rien autre chose qu'un très-mauvais lit de sangle, de vieux

---

[1] See below, p. 57.

[2] '. . . décédé subitement dans la vigne de Clamart d'Issy le 1er brumaire C.
Jacques Vinaugé, militaire invalide pensionné, natif d'Olivet (Loiret), 68 ans,
demeurant rue de la Contrescarpe (Arsenal) . . .' (procès-verbal du 6 brumaire an
IX).

[3] '. . . *Pierre Lorain*, peintre, environ 70 ans, 189 rue de l'Arbre-Sec (Gardes-
Françaises) . . . est mort d'une chute dans son escalier le jour d'hier . . . vers minuit
. . . qu'il est à notre connaissance que led. Lorrain étoit dans la plus grande indigence . . .' (procès-verbal du 14 messidor an VII).
An elderly *fille de confiance* 'nous a dit que le C. Bigot, demeurant à l'hospice
d'humanité, étant venu chez elle pour la voir, il est tombé mort subitement . . .
d'un coup de sang . . . *Cyr Bigot*, garçon . . . 52 ans . . . résidant en la maison de
Bicêtre comme indigent de Paris, [depuis] le 22 mars 1790' (procès-verbal du 9
ventôse an VIII). At least he died in company; possibly she was the one person he
knew in Paris; he was himself from the Eure-et-Loir.

[4] '. . . *Anne Juliette*, ancienne coiffeuse . . . une femme assise contre la porte sur
une chaise à gauche de la porte . . . il a été reconnu qu'elle étoit morte d'un coup de
sang, en ayant rendu beaucoup par le nez et la bouche dans un pot de chambre
qu'elle avait devant elle, et près duquel étoit un mouchoir ensanglanté . . . morte
dans un garni, 16 rue Honoré . . . depuis déjà trois jours . . .' (procès-verbal du
12 germinal an VIII).

souliers, quelques poteries, et de vieux haillons';[1] yet he was one of the relatively lucky ones, as the room, however sparse, seems to have been his at least to die in.[2]

The nine people murdered need not detain us at this stage, save to suggest that they appear rather as interlopers in the Basse-Geôle; and this is no doubt how the two *concierges* would have regarded them. Indeed, these display a somewhat ambivalent, even languid attitude towards what would often have appeared the clearest possible evidence of crimes of violence. They content themselves with such vague phrases as: *s'est brûlé la cervelle ou a été assassiné, aucun indice qu'il aît été assassiné*, and once they go even further, making the truly remarkable claim: *s'est noyé et a été assassiné*. In no case is the murderer identified (*sans qu'il aît été possible d'établir le nom du meurtrier* comes as a litany in these reports); nor is the slightest curiosity displayed as to possible motives. The excuse of the *juge de paix* and his two assistants would have been that, not being members of the criminal police, such speculations were outside their terms of reference.

Finally, if the documentation always gives such detailed information on the subject of clothing, it was because clothing, in the case of the drowned, would generally offer the only clue to identification. Laundry-marks, as we shall see, were more of a nuisance than a help in this respect, as the initials sewn on shirts and shifts in red and blue cotton so rarely correspond to those of the wearer, especially if she was a woman (at best, the second initial might be the same as the first letter of the surname, thus hinting at least at a family heirloom), and, indeed, as they often differ, on the same person, from one part of clothing to another. But, in the world of the poor, relatives, *intimes*, and neighbours would soon find their bearings in an intimate and unique geography of patches, mendings, tears, odd buttons, odd shoes, tunics, aprons, stitchings, and seams. The *suicidés* decided the time and place of their own deaths; clothing did not; it would go on and on. Such

---

[1] '. . . repêché aux Invalides *Jean-Edme-François Roy*, gagne-denier, 66 ans, natif de Venisy [Venizy] (Yonne), demeurant en garni, 4, rue Gervais-Lanseul (Cité) . . . sa logeuse ajoute que cet homme qui demande l'aumône est sujet à se prendre de boisson . . .' (procès-verbal du 8 fructidor an VIII).

[2] '. . . *Joseph Roche*, né le 23 avril 1783, mort subitement hier soir à 10 heures environ dans une chambre garnie . . . occupée par plusieurs garçons tailleurs [27 rue des Vieilles-Etuves] louée par le C. Wiethoff, tailleur . . . que depuis le 2 du courant led. Joseph Roche, natif de Clermont-Ferrand . . . étoit logé chez lui; le 14, il est rentré avant midi, se sentant mal; à 9 heures les autres garçons tailleurs, rentrant de leur journée, l'ont trouvé mort dans son lit . . .' (procès-verbal du 15 floréal an XI, D4 U1 31).

people carried very little with them through life, and most of that *on* them, day and night; clothing and the contents of pockets, including tools, probably often represented the entirety of wealth, and men who wore two or three pairs of trousers and several waistcoats, one on top of the other, did so, not so much to keep warm (we find bodies re-covered in summer so attired in several thicknesses of clothing, like once-walking wardrobes) as in an effort to preserve the totality of their wherewithal. How else could men and women, living in *garnis* in which there was no furniture, no drawer, nothing that could lock, ever keep *anything*?[1]

There thus arises a complete, if temporary, identity between cloth-ing, much of it inherited, or bought second-hand from the *Saint-Esprit*,[2] and wearer. But it is an identity which cannot last, even in the event of a more normal lifespan. The clothing, that, more than anything else—save accent, face, deformities, freckles, appearance, stature, bearing[3]—marks the individuality, the *uniqueness* of each of these people; having then seen them out, covered in decent modesty, it will distinguish, perhaps in a different sequence, another, or more probably, others (if there were always three or four *répondants* or *réclamants* come to the Basse-Geôle, both to answer for the body and to stake a claim on what it had left behind, it was no doubt not merely as a better guarantee of true identification, but each may have felt that he or she had a claim to a share of the clothing of the *identifié*). So clothing will detain us too at as much length as it had the two *concierges*, who knew what it was worth and could read into it something of the lives of those who had been its most recent temporary residents.

For, in a society existing before the introduction of cheap cottons and the consequent standardisation of working garments, clothing is

---

[1] Restif has in mind something much superior to the sort of furnished rooms likely to have been available to those who figure in the *procès-verbaux*, when he describes one such, in *Les Jolies-Femmes*: '. . . Il en choisit un qui donnait sur la rue . . . il eut l'assurance, d'être logé, couché, fourni de meubles, c'est-à-dire d'une table avec deux chaises, d'un miroir, d'un pot-à-l'eau, d'une cuvette, d'une ser-viette et d'un pot-de-chambre . . . on le pria de payer le demi-mois d'avance, d'écrire son nom sur un petit Registre . . .'

[2] '. . . La Fille n'avait que 2 petites robes, quelques deshabillers coquets, achetés au *Saintesprit*, et refaits . . .' '. . . Sa mise était mesquine, quoiqu'elle y mît de la prétention, en achetant au *saintesprit* du hasard coquet mais très-passé . . .' (ibid.).

[3] '. . . Elle marchait avec cette vivacité parisienne, si agréable, qui étonne les Arrivans . . .' '. . . Une démarche lascive qu'elle s'efforçait de rendre unie; mais elle ne réussissait qu'à augmenter le défaut qu'elle prétendait corriger . . .' (ibid.).

much more than purely functional: a covering against the ferocity and unpredictability of the elements, the wear and tear of long working hours,[1] and an assertion of public decency; it also expressed pride and individuality, a whole attitude to life, and one which seems to have carried beyond life, for some of the *suicidés* and *suicidées*—more indeed of the former than of the latter, as if the men were to stick to their vanity to the very steps of the grave—seem actually to have dressed up for their departure, as might a highwayman for his hanging, even to the extent of including such frills as lace cuffs, gloves, a coloured necktie high on the neck, embroidered *jabot*,[2] and top-boots over slippers. Among the eighteenth-century poor, *la couleur du temps* is reflected, or resisted, in the gay and variegated hues adopted by men who show a preference for a canary yellow, russet, bottle green, red and white, blue and white in stripes, bright checks, lustrous pale blues, shimmering plum, wine-coloured velvets, the favourite military combinations of blue and red, red and white, red and gold, a brilliant green with black facings, silver and gold frogs, mauve gloves, the fading, but still beautiful and evocative colours of *ancien régime* luxury and masculine pride, 'en habit de satin gorge-de-pigeon', and the frayed and fading colours of feminine artfulness of the 1780s, green or purple bodices, scarlet skirts, flowered patterns of blue, pink and white, dark blue picked out with white dots, the tender colours of female guile: 'bleu céleste', 'à petites raies, blanc-et-garance', 'une petite robe en fourreau, de soie gorge-de-pigeon' (again, a paling extreme luxury), 'une jolie ceinture argent-et-rose', 'rose-tendre', even deep black, a coquettish device to emphasise the fashionable paleness of skin.[3]

---

[1] 'En v'là une que je porte depuis 2 ans! & elle est encore comme neuve . . .' explains, in a Parisian accent, an artisan on the subject of a pair of *culottes de daim* (ibid.).

[2] '. . . Ne pouvant atteindre le visage ni les cheveux du Téméraire . . . elle déchira les jabots, les manchettes, les plus précieuses dentelles furent mises en loques . . .' The angry woman knew where best to strike at masculine vanity (ibid.).

Even an elderly *curé*, when setting up his newly hired servant, could offer him 'cent écus de gages, la table, 2 habits par an, 6 chemises: je vous monterai en boucles d'argent, chapeau, &ca'.

[3] '. . . un joli fourreau de bleu-céleste, garni en rose-tendre . . .' 'Sa robe était d'un brun qu'on nomme *puce* depuis quelques années . . . elle avait un tablier de tafetas noir, à bavette, qui rehaussait la blancheur naturelle de son teint . . .' 'Elle était en deshabiller juste, de tafetas rose, garni en vert . . .' 'Simple menuisière . . . parée avec une indienne à petites raies, blanc-et-garance, ou avec une toile à carreaux rouges . . .' 'Un beau Monsieur, en habit de satin gorge-de-pigeon . . .', ibid., and *Les Parisiennes*.

Of all contemporary observers, the one the best able to recapture the harlequin colours of the very poor, as they walked in rainbow clothing,[1] as if to defy death, always so close behind them, always dogging their brave footsteps, either in harmony with sun, shadow, and light, or in cheeky defiance of a Parisian November, is that discerning and incomparable memorialist of popular appearance and bearing, Francisco Goya: the hint of a smile on the face of a dark girl, her lustrous hair accentuated by a bright flower, the cheeky grin of an errand boy, the swaggering bearing of a soldier with a full moustache, the long red cloak of the doctor of medicine, the coloured straw-hat, to match her long shallow basket, of the laundress, the three-cornered hat, set at a rakish angle, of an ageing beau who has seen better times. And so one can appreciate why the dark garb affected by priests and monks should have been so readily accepted as components of popular anti-clericalism (though, too, the *costume de dévotion* could also be most seductive, on the right figure, as a thinly disguised invitation to acquaintanceship in the favourable intimacy of the shadow of an organ-loft or that of a spreading gothic pillar).[2] Those who dressed in dark clothing were birds of ill omen, the forerunners of ruin and death: *huissiers, hommes de loi, exempts,* funeral attendants, personages so often depicted in the still spontaneous popular prints of the early years of the Revolution, *crows*, and more sinister birds of prey.[3] It was all very well for that moralising misanthrope, an ageing Restif de la Bretonne, to envelop himself up to his nose in a long cloak the colour of night, his head covered by a vast shovel hat; but he was an eccentric, anxious to emphasise his apartness, a creature of the dark, walking

[1] '. . . Mon Mari est Maître Paumier; je suis moi-même un des meilleurs Joueuses de Paume & de Billard qu'il y ait au monde . . . Je m'habillais en petite veste blanche de bazin, avec un chapeau blanc rond garni de fleurs, des bas et hauts-de-chausse de soie d'une pièce, attachés à une jolie ceinture argent & rose, que j'avais autour des reins . . . Tous mes Joueurs devinrent mes Amans . . .' (*Les Jolies-Femmes*, VII, 'La Belle-Paumière').

[2] '[Il] . . . passa une partie de la matinée à Saintnicolas d'une manière édifiante; il était sous les orgues, en-méditation profonde, regardant néanmoins du coin de l'œil tout ce qui entrait dans l'église. Enfin, sur les 11 heures, Charlotte arriva seule . . .' *Les Jolies-Femmes*, V. See also: *Les Parisiennes*, '. . . elle était d'une beauté ravissante, sous le modeste costume de la dévotion.'

[3] If black was the colour of misfortune and death, there is some suggestion that *green* may have been the colour of crime, murder, and savagery. Two men suspected of being bandits, the one aged between 40 and 50, the other between 32 and 35, are described both as wearing hats: 'un chapeau rond couvert d'une toile cirée et *verte* et vêtu d'une redingote *verdâtre*', the other, 'un chapeau à 3 cornes et vêtu d'une redingote couleur *verdâtre* . . .' (A. N. BB 18 602, Ministre de la Justice, Somme, 7 ventôse an V).

through the silent, empty streets of the night, while even the *suicidables* of tomorrow either slept or kept to their rooms, *l'Hibou nocturne*.

Such then are the bare, yet allusive, ingredients of a dossier uniquely complete, and at the same time containing an extraordinary variety of information, both direct, peripheral, and inductive, for anyone who is prepared not only to give each sad *procès-verbal* a fairer hearing than its hasty scrawl would make it appear to deserve (the *juge de paix* no doubt rightly considered that the living had a better claim on his time and his patience than the dead, and that it was sheer bad luck that the Basse-Geôle, the central point for all the drowned in Paris, should have fallen within his jurisdiction), but to read beyond its repetitive and life-lessly formal language in order to pick up and scrutinise each item of clothing and each scrap of peripheral information that it offered, in-cluding descriptions of bandages, birth-marks, warts, freckles, and wounds, even to speculate on the reason for the absence of such other voluntarily imposed distinguishing marks as tattoos (an absence that may well have a *negative* social value), in an effort at least to reconstruct what may have gone before the last fatal decision. How many of these 270 or so suicides, while still alive, and not yet *objects* laid out in display, awaiting a tag, a label permitting them to be parcelled off and disposed of, had gone through all the lengthy rigmarole of dressing—assuming of course that they had ever completely undressed, a luxury more likely to be reserved to the well-to-do and the well-born, to those who had servants to lace them up from behind, a luxury that is hinted at in the popular wonder expressed at a series of rapid changes of clothing as shouted by a barker outside a theatre in order to attract an audience ('changing into a suit of black and silver, he draws his sword on . . .')[1] —in the absolute certitude that this would be the last time that they would pull on their stockings, buckle up their shoes, pull on their top-boots, lace up their bodice, put on one skirt over another, and yet another over that, gird themselves in three pairs of breeches and two waistcoats, adjust their neckties?[2] How many may have committed suicide simply because the river was where it was, and because it was so much easier to act there and then,[3] get it over with (though perhaps

---

[1] For a marvellous description of the barkers outside the theatres of the Boulevard du Temple, under the July Monarchy, see Eugen Weber, *Peasants into Frenchmen*, p. 228: 'Mr Pompey will change costume 12 times. He will carry off the Commander's daughter dressed in a frogged jacket, and will be struck down in a spangled suit.'

[2] See Note D, p. 107.

[3] '. . . En sortant de l'Hôpital, Rose ne vit devant elle qu'une solitude im-mense: toutes les portes des Honnêtes-gens lui étaient fermées . . . Il n'y a plus

with also a very slight hope of rescue),[1] rather than to return to lodgings in search of a weapon, or to set up the not entirely simple apparatus of self-strangulation? But how indeed to avoid so many 'might haves', 'must have beens', and 'must haves', when the principal witnesses have condemned themselves to silence?

So the suicides must have pride of place, not only because they are the most numerous in a group otherwise gathered together by accident, old age, illness, and murder, but also because they alone pose most of the problems, whether as a mute gesture of private hopelessness and despair, or as an unheard protest against public injustice and cruelty. Traditional popular opinion would have had it so, since even the suicide of a female servant, in the year after Waterloo, was considered, by those who knew how to read into the public mind, to be an event of such considerable importance and of such exemplary moral value, something in fact to be avoided, like eating mushrooms on a picnic in December, as to gain admittance to that pantheon of popular wisdom, *Le Véritable Almanach de Liége*, for 1816.[2] Suicide, being an expression of will, must offer some commentary both on the life that went before and on the entourage of the victim. But accidental death,

---

d'ouvrage pour moi chez les Tapissiers; je ne pourrai trouver de place pour être femme-de-chambre, pas même pour être servante; *qui répondra de moi?* . . . en fesant le trajet de l'Hôpital à la porte Saint-Bernard . . . en entrant dans Paris, elle jeta les yeux sur le pont de la Tournelle . . . Un parti se présente . . . Malheureuse, va sur ce pont, & précipite-toi dans la Seine; c'est le plus court . . . je ne saurois te peindre . . . l'excès de mon désespoir. Je me serais donné la mort, si des sentimens de religion & de philosophie ne m'eussent retenue . . .' Restif, *Les Jolies-Femmes*, IX. 'Qui répondra de moi?' an eloquent suggestion of the importance of having a *répondant(e)* in life, even more than in death.

[1] See Note E, p. 107.

[2] The *Almanach de Liége* for 1816 carries the following item of news: 'M. V**** revenoit au mois d'août de sa campagne; il trouve, non plus sa cuisinière à la maison, mais sur la table, une bague, 2 boucles d'oreille et ce billet. *Le 71 me conduit au tombeau, quand vous recevrez cette lettre, je serai dans le canal de la Villette.* En effet le corps de cette malheureuse fut retrouvé à la Morgue. Elle avait, entraînée par sa fatale passion, mis en gage quantité d'objets appartenant à ses maîtres, et n'avoit pu supporter ses remords . . .' The didactic purpose of the item is emphasised by the heading under which it appears: 'Effets de la Loterie'. The same almanac, for the year 1814, tells the sad story of an 'honnête famille de Castel Sarrazin [qui] vient d'offrir un nouvel exemple du danger de se nourrir sans choix de champignons . . .' The family had sat down to eat the mushrooms, on a December afternoon, in the shade of a poplar. The mother and her younger son, aged seven, had died. The almanac concludes: 'Il est reconnu que tous les champignons qui viennent après les premières gelées de l'hiver sont vénéneux: cette connoissance est générale dans la campagne; et il a fallu que cette malheureuse famille l'ignorât.'

death from natural causes, and, of course, murder (something enveloped in the dreadful prestige of rarity and darkness, so many murders being discoverable at dawn, on the opening of shutters, doors, and windows, and again, an event sufficiently important for it to be commented on and embalmed in an even older favourite of popular literature, *Le Messager Boîteux de Berne*, in the memorable year of 1796)[1] are likewise not to be lightly dismissed, merely because they were *not* acts of will. There is a great deal of good sense in the choice of almanacs will give more space to the fact that a baby died of burns, because it had been left unattended, that a child had fallen out of the window, because its mother had gone out shopping, or—worse—to have a drink, that a little boy had been suffocated, because again its mother had gone off to meet her lover (it is always the *mother* at fault, always the heading *Négligence coupable d'une mère* that will introduce a story that, however repetitive, still seems worth telling, year after year, in these wonderfully hardy annuals)[2] than to great battles or changes of régime, and that will place the dead child at the same exalted level as the death of a prince.

Dying was an important business two hundred years ago, as it must always be in a civilised society. It is consoling to discover that an urban society as allegedly brutal as that of eighteenth-century Paris should never have become habituated to suicide, regarding it, on the contrary, as something worse than murder, and that it was prepared to spend at least a little time on the administrative formalities arising from the sudden death of children or adolescents, and to give details about the last activities of an old man or an old woman, suddenly overtaken by death, while walking in the street, while sitting sociably in a public place, or while lying, untended in a closed room. Very occasionally our documentation will even allow such humble people the rare luxury of last words, or something murmured in the snow, something whispered to a flustered *gargotier*, somewhat put out by such an unexpected break in the routine of his day and causing him to keep impatient customers waiting a little, perhaps at the height of trade; for sudden death could

[1] See Note F, p. 110.

[2] *Le véritable almanach de Liége pour l'an bissextil 1816*, 'Anecdotes . . . Douai, 1 Novembre 1814*. Il y a 2 jours que dans cette ville, une mère laisse imprudemment un enfant de 2 à 3 ans dans la cave qu'elle habitoit, auprès d'un réchaud dans lequel il y avoit un brasier. Le feu a pris aux vêtements de cet enfant; ils étoient déjà consumés lorsque la mère est rentrée. Malgré les secours les plus empressés apportés par M le Dr. Gromer, l'enfant a rendu le dernier soupir 2 ou 3 heures après, dans les douleurs les plus affreuses. Nouvelle victime de l'imprudence avec laquelle certaines mères perdent momentanément de vue leurs enfans en bas âge.'

be very inconsiderate. Finally, perhaps an unexpected bonus to be derived from a long and patient research into the *procès-verbaux* of *la mort subite*, is that the silent dead, through no fault of theirs, apart from merely being dead in a manner not entirely convenient, not respecting the accepted rules of decorum on the important subject of departure from life, may tell us a great deal more about the living, so that four hundred dead can witness, in a number of unexpected ways, for as many as fifteen hundred people who survived them.

II

BEYOND THE 'DOSSIER'

'His aspect reminded me of something I had seen—something funny I had seen somewhere. As I manoeuvred to get alongside, I was asking myself, "What does this fellow look like?" Suddenly I got it. He looked like a harlequin. His clothes had been made of some stuff that was brown holland probably, but it was covered with patches all over, with bright patches, blue, red, and yellow—patches on the back, patches on the front, patches on elbows, on knees; coloured binding around his jacket, scarlet edging at the bottom of his trousers; and the sunshine made him look extremely gay and wonderfully neat withal, because you could see how beautifully all this patching had been done. . . .'

Joseph Conrad, *Heart of Darkness*

'. . . That his wife should hit upon the precaution of sewing the boy's address inside his overcoat was the last thing Mr Verloc would have thought of. One can't think of everything. That was what she meant when she said that he need not worry if he lost Stevie during their walks. She had assured him that the boy would turn up alright. Well, he had turned up, with a vengeance!'

Joseph Conrad, *The Secret Agent*

'. . . Mr Verloc was not frightful to behold. He looked comfortable. Moreover, he was dead. Mrs Verloc entertained no vain delusions on the subject of the dead. Nothing brings them back, neither love nor hate. They can do nothing to you. They are as nothing. Her mental state was tinged by a sort of austere contempt for that man who had let himself be killed so easily. He had been the master of a house, the husband of a woman, the murderer of her Stevie. And now he was of no account in every respect. He was of less practical account than the clothing on his body, than his overcoat, than his boots—than that hat lying on the floor. He was nothing. He was not worth looking at. . . .'

Joseph Conrad, *The Secret Agent*

(i)

The *juge de paix* and the historian

'. . . *Charles-Vincent d'Aubigny*, garçon limonadier, natif d'Antilly (Oise), domicilié chez son frère, Jacques d'Aubigny, limonadier, 618 rue du Contrat-Social, disparu depuis 15 jours, cadavre repêché le 7 près le port de la Grenouillière, vêtu d'une carmagnole de nanquin rayé violette, d'un gilet rouge de soie, d'un autre de bazin piqué, d'un pantalon pareil à ladite carmagnole . . . d'un soulier pointu . . . cadavre reconnu par Jacques d'Aubigny, limonadier, comme étant son frère germain. . . .'

Procès-verbal en date du 8 brumaire an VI[1]

---

[1] '. . . le C. Paulin Croy, marinier . . . demeurant ordinairement à Compiègne . . . qu'il venoit de retirer de l'eau un cadavre de sexe masculin . . . sur la berge . . . près des Bains Poitevins . . . avons trouvé sur lui une carte de sûreté délivrée le 7 nivôse de l'an 2 à la Section de la Fontaine de Grenelle . . . qu'il est natif d'Antilly, département de l'Oise, âgé de 26 ans, demeurant rue de Beaune No 766 et s'appelle *Charles-François Vincent D'Aubigny* . . .' On the body, 4 francs 10 sols in cash, a passport delivered 30 Fructidor Year IV by the municipality of Antilly, various papers, a pair of leather gloves. His body is recognised by his brother, Jacques-Pierre D'Aubigny, *limonadier*, and by his brother-in-law, Paillon, captain, 2me bataillon, 20me demi-brigade (D10 U1 7, juge de paix de la Section de la Fontaine de Grenelle, procès-verbal du 7 brumaire an VI).

THE *juge de paix* of the Division du Muséum had, as we have seen, among his other tasks, to keep an up-to-date count of those who died violently within his watery domain, or just inland, with a view to identification. An unidentified corpse, however poorly clad, represented a vague threat to a *société policée* that sought above all to be able to account for all its citizens, living, or but recently dead. An unknown body was an enigma, and so a problem: it might conceivably be that of some famous villain sought all over the Republic, though the likelihood was that it would be someone of such little consequence as hardly to be worthy of even the brief attention of a minor judicial official. Still, as long as there was doubt, there would be some cause for alarm.

For one thing, *cadavre masculin inconnu*, or *cadavre féminin inconnu*, illustrated the serious limits placed on the effectiveness of government; and if there were a stream of such, they might be seen as the forerunners of some great seasonal or cyclical crisis, as they must indeed have seemed to such consistent readers in death and disaster as Bouille and Daude, when the numbers presumably began to increase in the course of the spring and summer of the Years II, III, and IV.[1] On the other hand, a body, once identified, became a rather undesirable object that had to be disposed of, especially in summer, as speedily as possible.

Such concern to have the bodies in his care identified, whether by family, friends, neighbours, or workmates, would not spring, on the part of the *juge de paix*, from any desire to put these out of their misery nor to offer them at least a few words of consolation. Once recognised, they could be taken out of this dangerous limbo of temporary anonymity, back into ordered society, and their clothes at least could be returned to relatives or friends. Identified, even suicides and victims of murder were reinstated in the safe world of a well-kept *état-civil*. The *juge de paix* and his two acolytes were not sentimentalists, and it was not their function to attempt to feel their way backwards in a life so wilfully terminated and to probe into possible motivations. Even more so for the victims of accidents and those who had died, however suddenly, a natural death. A corpse was a corpse; the fact of death was undeniable; it was not for them to speculate whether an elderly pauper had died of cold, or of starvation, or simply of old age and fatigue. Being men of habit, well-versed in their peculiar specialisation, they may merely have had cause to comment on the weekly, monthly,

[1] See Note G, p. 111.

seasonal, or yearly fluctuations in these grisly journeys downstream: 'rather more than usual for this time of the year', 'a lot of May girls again', 'they seem to be getting younger', 'that is the second well-dressed man in a week', 'another red-head', 'another hernia, a woman this time', 'nasty sores on the legs again', 'February, the river is high, and the soldiers are back', 'August and its crop of swimmers'. And they must also have been aware that, in the six-year period covered by their records (though there must presumably have existed, at one time, similar records both for the revolutionary period proper, and for the subsequent one), annual suicide by drowning, far from staying at a fairly constant figure, was in fact steadily increasing, from the Year VI to the Year IX. What they might have made of that we do not know: probably not very much, as the previous seven years of random re-volutionising would have conditioned them to the expectation of every type of violence, both public and private, and because, taken up with a day-to-day count, they were unlikely to have perceived the broader sweep.

All eighteenth-century judicial and police authorities were particu-larly sensitive to the subject of death in the open, because the spectacle offered by sudden and violent death was believed to be dangerously inducive of imitation.[1] It was also a matter of simple human dignity; even the patient effort to put a name on a body, and to escape from the indecent bleakness of anonymity—something even more shocking than, but very much akin to, nudity[2] (the two would go together)— was not only conditioned by concern for *la chose publique*; it represented

---

[1] D4 U1 31, procès-verbal du 13 fructidor an X, commre. des Marchés: a woman of 27, *fille de confiance*, falls down dead at 3 p.m. in the place des Innocents. The body is taken to the Hospice de l'humanité, where it is refused admission; so it is brought to 47 rue de la Truanderie, the girl's address; but, on reaching the entrance, a citizen, coming down the staircase, 's'est écrié: *Citoyens, ne montez pas; Madame Baron* [the girl's employer] *n'y est pas et s'est opposée à ce que le corps fût monté* . . . voulant éviter tout scandale et par respect pour les morts, avons fait rapporter et déposer le corps . . . dans le bâtiment de la halle aux draps . . .'

[2] There is an obvious connection between nudity, disgrace, and the rigours of punishment; the mother of a young man condemned to the galleys writes drama-tically to the Minister of Justice: '. . . Le bruit des chaînes, des marteaux, annonce le pitoyable aspect de *ces infortunés à demi-nuds*, attachés l'un à l'autre par des colliers de fer, et bientôt exposés aux injures de l'aide et à celles de ces hommes barbares qui les conduisent et qui pour les intimider croient de se rendre terribles en affectant un air farouche, soutenus par des propos grossiers durs et insolens . . .' (A.N. BB 18 602, Ministre de la Justice, Oise). The authorities of the Eure refer, in Brumaire Year IV, to the wretched condition of the English prisoners-of-war held in Evreux gaol: 'Leurs vêtements sont en lambeaux, ils sont nuds pieds, malades, et dans un état qui fait peine . . .' (A.N. BB 18 297, Eure).

at least a modest tribute to the uniqueness of a human being that had only recently been alive. Only the body of someone defeated in a state of civil war could be rejected as a mere piece of dirty débris, an enemy not even deserving the minimal luxury of a name and a covering. If they could have—and indeed they tried very hard—the two *concierges* would have liked to have shuttled back the bloody remains of the poor house-painter from north-central Paris, a fanatic or a victim killed in the *affaire de Grenelle*, to where it had come from initially, that is to the military, responsible in any case for its bloody condition (see below, pp. 89–90).

Within its chosen limits, eighteenth-century urban society was residually merciful, and the peculiar pair who presided over the temporary resting-place of the drowned, the shot, the hanged, the murdered, and the merely dead, were not solely motivated by administrative concern to have everything neatly tabulated (though their achievement in this respect is highly commendable, only about a score of more than 400 bodies totally eluding identification) and to have their books in order—certainly in better order than those of the living in the *registres* of the *logeurs*—but they seem also to have been aware that they were in a position to write the last word about those who came their way, and that their *procès-verbaux* were almost something more: brief epitaphs on people most of whom had only once achieved public recognition, by the form of their death. A chronicle, however, of epitaphs, in which almost everything was likely to be repetitive, taking up, 400 times or more, the same short story at the same ending, is a chronicle that allows only a very limited range of impressionism or fantasy, and which entirely excludes the unexpected, if only because we too, like the *concierges* and the *juge*, come in after the curtain has gone down. If indeed only the corpses had been involved, and, of course, what had been their clothing, then Daude and Bouille would have left us little more than a long list of names and Christian names—and even the poorest were rich in these, three or four, as if to compensate for inherited deprivation by a wealth of saints (especially in the case of the small drowned girls)—occupations, birthplaces, ages, marital status, addresses, time, place, and manner of self-destruction, accident, sudden death, or murder, time of departure from home (or when last seen, which comes to much the same thing: the *concierges* were particularly concerned to follow this one up), date, time, and place of recovery from the river.

What they also provide us, obviously because they thought this was of the greatest importance, almost as if they themselves believed that Clothing Made the Man (or the Woman)[1] was a detailed analysis of clothing that, however varied in range of colour, in the patchwork of constant repair, and in the confused code posed by apparently unrelated laundry-marks and initials (revealing perhaps only the fact that a shirt had passed through many hands after the original owner, or that it had covered more than one generation of the same family, and more than one member of the same generation, including sisters as well as brothers, or that it had been sold at a loss to a *revendeuse*, in order to meet some pressing need, or that it had been stolen, not once, but twice, or thrice, probably as it passed through the hands of a succession of laundrywomen), had generally in common very poor quality and a weariness even greater, because spread over many more years, than that of people normally engaged in occupations involving very long hours, great physical effort, and very little sleep, and all in appalling conditions. 'Torn', 'darned', 'stitched together', 'worn down to the seam', 'holed', 'heel-less', 'out at the elbows', 'out at the knees', 'patched', 'reinforced with leather squares', 'worn through at the seat', 'letting in water', are words that represent, in graphic terms, an economy of fairly desperate expedients, and a daily effort merely to keep going a little longer: another week, a couple of months, until the spring, until Michaelmas, until Trinity, until All Souls' Day (a sort of affirmation of the will to live). The only difference would be that, whereas most of the working population would be similarly clothed, these unfortunates, despite the darns and patches—small works of art and ingenuity, the illustration of loving care on the part of someone, the example too of a strong will to survive—that covered them till the end with the rags of decency—and the darns and patches represented, on the part of those who had indeed brought out thimble, needle, and thread to complete them, a very modest claim on the future, at least for the clothes, if not for the wearer, a tiny gesture of optimism and concern—had, all at once, and for reasons that must generally remain impenetrable, given up the struggle.

So the *juge de paix* and his assistants have, for one reason or other, done rather well not only by their dead clientèle, but also by any historian prepared to travel with them. In so far as they display a hasty, bluff, and rather unencumbered humanity, the historian should emu-

---

[1] '. . . Dans ce Pays-ci, on ne regarde que l'écorce, & si la Fille du Bourreau, ou d'un homme exécuté, paraissait dans un cercle avec des charmes & des diamans à côté de la modeste Femme d'un Gentilhomme qui aurait servi l'Etat, mal-vêtue, fût-elle jolie, la première auroit tous les hommages, & même toute la considération . . .' (Restif, *Les Jolies-Femmes*, VI).

late them. And in so far as they attempt to fill in the many blanks in the previously unknown life of a drowned man or girl, of a murdered shop-girl or female servant, of a murdered army officer, of a murdered man in the drink trade, of a lonely old man or of a desperate old woman, or of someone dying all at once in company, by taking a careful stock of even the minutest objects that have accompanied them until then— including broken ones, no doubt then retained for sentimental reasons[1] —and of body marks, wounds, freckles, the tilt of a nose, and so on, he should follow their careful, if hurried, example.

But at this point, the *juge* and the historian will part company; the *iuge* will go on to his next assignation: another body, and another after that, and on and on he will go, till retirement (the most likely, for, if, during these years, there is a constant turnover of *commissaires de police*, a post dangerously exposed to the shifting politics of the Year II, Thermidor, and the Directory, the less politicised *juges de paix* are often revealed as having very long runs indeed in their assigned quarters), dismissal, or a welcome promotion inland, away from the riverside, delivers him from the treadmill of the Basse-Geôle. The *juge*, who has his own career to consider, will be looking forward; he may even be in search of a clientèle a little more expressive and more varied than these mute objects which take up so much of his time. The his-torian, on the other hand, has only just started out on an uncertain journey at the moment when he first notes the details of a *procès-verbal*, or the minor differences between this one and another. From there, he will attempt to move backwards, beyond the terrible barrier imposed by the fact of self-destruction or sudden death, in an effort to fill out a life generally incomplete (though some of the old people might be said to have lived out their hard days), cut off, not just with a random collection of objects in everyday use, but with words, feelings, people, a childhood, a birthplace, the number of years previously spent in the city, companionship, marriage, whether terminated or still involving cohabitation, widowhood, absence of a partner, illness, itineraries in

---

[1] The historian should be careful never to underestimate both the sentimental value of small objects, even if they are broken and have long since ceased serving any practical purpose, and their value as tiny, yet exemplary, witnesses to a way of life, to a form of provincialism, to a regional identity, and to a period in social history. It is something that has been very well captured by Alistair Horne, in his history of the Algerian War (*A Savage War of Peace*, London, 1977), when, describing the exodus of the *pied noir* population, he writes: 'In Bab-el-Oued great pyres were lit in the street as the *pieds noirs* . . . burned . . . the souvenirs from happier times—aquatints of the Conquest, framed photos of *grand maman*, of family picnics to celebrate the "breaking of the *mouna*" . . .'

life, and so on. Very rarely indeed it may even be possible for him to relate these blurred, fudged lives to public events and to the direct experience of history.

It is a journey that requires unlimited curiosity, and endless search for detail that may at first seem trivial, and an appreciation of the strangeness of objects oddly assorted, picked up as it were off a vast rubbish heap, rather like a historian's visit to a still unfashionable, and totally unselfconscious *marché aux puces* before bric-à-brac became modish. He will then walk in a landscape formed of a bizarre assortment of juxtapositions: death of a *journalière* lodging in the rue de la Vieille-Tuerie, on the steps of the Basse-Geôle,[1] death in the rue des Morfondus, death in the rue de la Mortellerie, as if sudden death had been endowed with an impish sense of humour; a severed head discovered in a gutter, rue du Petit-Musc; a Saturday death in the bathhouse, watch on the hook.[2] Death is sometimes even a jolly fellow, creeping up behind the elderly pensioner, as he enjoys a rare Monday visit to a *marchand de vin*, tripping up the widow on her way to see an unwelcoming relative, thus spared embarrassment, and luring on his travelling companion, to the Palace of the King (*soldat médecin*) with the promise of fine fare, only the very best, wine only of the most exquisite quality (*du vin bouché*), tobacco *au choix*, accompanied by the faintly derisive and diabolically military tune of *Joseph*'s surrendered ten-franc violin.

[1] '. . . mort subite d'une femme environ 30 ans, vêtue d'une camisole lilas rayée très mauvaise, un mauvais jupon blanc, un bas bleu et blanc déchiré, l'autre jambe nue, et remplie de mal, des sabots, et un petit bonnet rond, trouvée sur les marches du grand escalier du Châtelet . . .' (procès-verbal en date du 2 nivôse an IV).
See also: '*Françoise Sévrey*, femme Chéret, journalière demeurant 7 rue de la Vieille-Tuerie (Arcis), 33 ans, native de Châtillon-sur-Indre, décédée subitement ce matin Cour du ci-devant Châtelet, qu'une goutte remontée de l'estomac est la cause du décès . . .' (procès-verbal du 11 vendémiaire an VI).
[2] A *garçon baigneur* reports, 25 Pluviôse Year IX (Saturday, 4 February 1801), 'qu'un particulier qui étoit venu en jourd'hui pour prendre un bain . . . aux bains dits Vigier, en face de la grille des Tuileries, venoit de décéder dans sa baignoire . . . où étant, côté des hommes, et entré dans une petite chambre à gauche, No 6 . . . avons trouvé dans une baignoire placée à la gauche dud. cabinet un cadavre de sexe masculin mort dans lad. baignoire encore remplie d'eau . . . une partie de la tête hors de l'eau . . . avons trouvé accroché à un clou posé entre les 2 robinets une petite montre dans sa boëte d'or, gioché mouvement de Lepautre à Paris . . . un petit flacon de crystal avec bouton en or, led. flacon contenant de l'eau de mélisse . . . un vieux chapeau rond à haute forme . . . un manteau de drap bleu. . . .' The dead man, who suffered from epilepsy, was a *notaire public*, aged 37. who had come presumably to enjoy his Saturday bath (A.D. Seine D1 U1 35, juge de paix des Tuileries).

It is like writing a series of biographies *backwards*, from beyond the grave, the principal witness, Our Hero, a corpse well on the way to decomposition, even beyond the reach of recognition, and so merely a bundle of miscellaneous clothing, never the *complete* outfit, the walking-out fetch-me-down, always out of step, out of joint, shuffling along *clopin-clopant*, one shoe missing, one stocking only, and that torn, the other leg bare, several layers of waistcoat, but no jacket, no topcoat (only three corpses are revealed as wearing a *redingote*), as if one had gone to death as one might have gone to work, in shirt-sleeves and apron, suitable enough in the case of people whose every gesture while alive had been that of hard, continuous, physical effort, as if one had gone to an untidy death untidily, incorrectly dressed, a button off here and there, or buttons of different material, three brass, four cloth, one shoe with a buckle, the other without, a bundle laid out as for inspection, necktie, shirt, and waistcoat at the top end, red or blue *ceinture*, red woollen cummerbund, or leather belt, closed by a lion clasping its tail holding up breeches or trousers,[1] stockings, gaiters, shoes, or slippers at the bottom, thus showing up what is missing, the tattered, stumbling, dragging armies of defeat.

Death and suicide, as we shall see, will also uncover a double, even a triple, network: family, neighbourhood, conformity of work and conformity of leisure: a carter among carters, a laundress among laundresses and laundrymen, a *garçon baigneur* among others engaged in that watery and soapy pursuit, horsy people among horsy people, the extensive yet impenetrable world of the stables covering so very much of the terrain of the city, the workshop and the wine-shop recreated and repeopled on the other side of death, leaving the observer with the troubled feeling: 'if only so much concern could have been displayed earlier', as if the assurance of all this verbal cosseting, the pre-awareness of a collective absorption so protective, and so apparently affectionate and well-meaning, might have protected at least the potential suicide from the decision of withdrawal. For people who were mostly to be buried hastily at the expense of the city, and in the absence of any cere-

---

[1] '. . . *Jacques-François Patar*, cordonnier, natif de Paris, 41 ans, domicilié quai de Gêvres 6 (Arcis), marié . . . une chemise marquée *F.P.*, un gilet rond de molleton gris, une culotte noire de satin turc, une paire de bas de fil gris, une paire de s. à c., une paire de boucles à jarretières en argent, une serpillière devant lui attachée à un crochet en cuivre représentant un lion, un mouchoir de poche marqué *F.P.*, et une tabatière de carton couleurs mélangées . . . cadavre reconnu par son beau-frère, Antoine Duriez, laveur de cendres, rue du Haut-Moulin, division de la Cité, par sa sœur et par son neveu . . .' (procès-verbal du 22 prairial an VII).

mony, religious or otherwise, the *procès-verbaux* habitually take the form of a roll of attendance at a memorial service.

Clearly, if such attention means anything at all, apart of course from a natural concern to put oneself right with the authorities—and even a sudden death in the street, much more a suicide, could not but be a most undesirable embarrassment to those concerned, if only because it brought them within range of official attention (something always best to be avoided, and also because awkward questions might be asked, and the living made to prove their identity as well as the dead)—and perhaps also the desire to make sure that nothing remained that might be worth claiming, many of these *suicidés*, or the former inmates of charitable institutions who fell down dead in public, after having spent a lifetime attempting not to draw attention to themselves, must have been much richer, if not in material things—and the full range of such meagre *bilans* offered to us can leave us in no doubt as to that—at least in companionship and concern.

We will return to this elusive problem of sociability, in the urban, even the street, context, when we turn our attention beyond the corpses to those who come to vouch for them, to answer for them, *comparants* and *répondants*, those too who hint at the existence of a closely observed society, wide open to the street, or actually on the street, the outer walls and connecting ones torn down, the windows employed as points of observation and spyholes, the window-sills (*accoudoirs*, positions of cushioned comfort and protracted ease) as observatories on to the street and the passer-by and on to the well of the staircase, or, indeed, on to other windows within range of a penetrating glance, the warm-weather observers even moving forward into the street itself, by putting out chairs, or sitting on doorsteps.[1] And one might learn from them the accepted manner of leaning, as if in danger of losing one's footing, so as to induce a closer approach, a contrived stumble that will bring out the rapid protective arm,[2] the exploitation of passing

---

[1] '. . . un soir que j'étais assise devant la porte avec ma mère, je vis passer un carosse, qui s'arrêta, en se rangeant si près de notre porte, que nous fumes obligées de nous lever. Ma mere rentra . . . emportant sa chaise . . .' (Restif, *Les Jolies-Femmes*, II). '. . . J'avais pour usage, en été surtout les dimanches & fêtes, de m'asseoir, pour avoir plus de frais, sur la trappe de la cave entr'ouverte où l'on plaçait un banc . . .' (ibid.).

[2] '. . . Si tu es avec lui quelque part, & que tu lui donnes le bras, tu affecteras de petites frayeurs, suivant l'occasion. Je l'ai enchanté, un jour, au monticule du *Jardin-du-Roi*, en n'osant descendre que presque dans ses bras . . .' (Restif, *Les Parisiennes*). A trick still in use, on the way down the steep bank at the top of which is planted the famous *cèdre de Jussieu*, in the Jardin des Plantes.

traffic, as it sweeps close to the walls of houses and shops, in order to
get closer to someone,[1] at least within whispering range, the knowledge that certain streets—the rue de la Sorbonne, for instance[2]—were
quieter than most, with few passers-by and, so, less observed; and the
habit of Parisian males, at least when beyond reach of their own
quarters, openly to express their admiration to the backs of girls whom
they pass or whom they are following, thus making full use of the
anonymity of a city, once past the boundaries of quarter.[3]

A meticulous and, in its subtle way, an ordered society, closely
governed by the relative equality of conditions—a haberdasher for a
stationer, a grocer for a butcher—the jealous concern for honour, a
society in which every gesture has its assigned place, in which every
invitation is fraught with significance—none more so than to be asked
to Sunday lunch, a firm commitment on the part of the inviter[4]—in
which there are always set rules for meeting people, set attitudes to be
struck when met, set places: churches, *quinconces*, shrubberies, the
innermost sanctum of a maze, a small clearing set with moss-covered
mounds bearing a trickling fountain and a small cherub armed with
bow and arrows[5] in which to meet, small armies of intermediaries,
outriders, intelligence officers, scouts, negotiators, without whose help
such meetings could never take place in the first place, nor even a name
be given to a face, an address given to a name, doors left open, keys
provided for doors that are locked, secret entrances, sliding panels,
convenient cupboards, open front rooms, a rigmarole of crossings

---

[1] '. . . une cérémonie lugubre, & fort dispendieuse, qui passait par notre rue, lui
en fournit l'occasion, il vint à côté de notre porte, & s'approcha de moi . . .' (Restif,
Les Jolies-Femmes, II).

[2] '. . . & dans la rue de *Sorbonne*, qui est toujours solitaire, il hasarda un compliment . . .' (op. cit., I).

[3] '. . . je recevais toujours en rue quelque compliment ou quelque parole-libre,
comme cela nous arrive à toutes; dans cette grande Ville, où l'on ne se connaît pas,
chacun dit sans honte ce qu'il pense . . .' (op. cit., V).

[4] Such an invitation on the part of the parents of the girl is the first step before
discussing the actual conditions of marriage.

[5] '. . . Faustine entra seule sous un berceau, qui termine l'allée en face de la
maison; ainsi de Consolent l'aperçut d'abord; mais il prit par une contr'allée. La
Jeune personne qui voulut l'éprouver, sortit du berceau, & fut se cacher dans un
bosquet de rosiers & de lilas fort touffus, où il étoit impossible de la voir, à moins
d'y entrer. Au milieu de ce bosquet était une petite grotte de coquillages, où
se trouvait un lit de mousse; les branches des rosiers y entraient par différentes
ouvertures pratiquées exprès & leurs roses couraient en guirlandes audessus
du lit, dont un petit Amour fermait le chevet, avec son carquois plein de
flèches. Ce fut dans cet endroit charmant que se cacha Faustine. Elle se mit sur le
lit de mousse, & feignit de dormir . . .' (op. cit., IX).

over barriers erected to preserve a strict segregation of the orders:
indeed, a world of gesture and of speech[1] almost as formalised as the
carefully repeated, yet gradually changing, now advancing, now re-
treating, now approaching, now withdrawing, steps of a minuet.

---

[1] Especially the mocking tone, *le ton taquin*, of a pretty and provoking woman:
'. . . Il se démasqua le premier . . . l'Automate fut ému (autant que peut l'être une
machine) . . . l'Automate, comme tous ses Pareils, étoit avantageux . . . quoique
machine, il avait des sens . . .' (op. cit., IX), and Restif is very fond of putting such
words as *Automate* and *Téméraire* in the mouths of his not-so-virtuous girls.

(ii)

The calendar of
suicide and sudden death:
emulation and opportunity

'. . . *Marin Prosper Arȝon*, marchand peaussier, natif de Paris, 47 ans, rue de la Jussienne . . . disparu depuis le 11 à 10 heures du matin . . . que ledit cadavre a été trouvé suicidé dans le bois de Boulogne . . . sur lui, une chemise marquée *P.A.*, un habit redingotte de molleton gris, un gilet de nankin jaune, une culotte de drap gris garnie de peau, une paire de bas de coton chiné, une paire de souliers à cordons et une cravate de mousseline bleu et blanc . . . le cadavre reconnu par trois particuliers dont un, Pierre Courant, est marchand pelletier, rue Saint-Denis, hôtel du Grand Cerf 62 . . .'

Procès-verbal du 17 prairial an VIII

'. . . *Augustin Rémy Auvert*, peintre élève de David, natif de Paris . . . 19 ans et ½, fils mineur de Nicolas Auvert, rentier, 134 rue du faubourg Martin, disparu depuis le 3, 3 heures de relevé . . . il a été trouvé au bas d'une des tours du temple de la Raison (Cité) sur les 4 heures de relevé, qu'il avoit sur lui une chemise, une cravate de soie brune, un gilet de velours rouge, un pantalon de drap gris, une paire de bas de laine . . . le cadavre a été reconnu par son père chez qui il demeuroit . . .'

Procès-verbal en date du 4 ventôse an VIII

As if in hidden response to such cloying familiarities and unwritten collective orthodoxies, suicide itself, especially suicide by drowning, seems to witness to a form of sociability, however tenuous, both as to time and to place, even building up its own momentum of imitation and emulation. Often one suicide will secrete another, there are suicides with the same surname—and that an uncommon one—though the exact relationship is not indicated (it was hardly the concern of the *juge* to look into such niceties and to follow up such hints, as he would have indignantly rejected any suggestion by the Minister of Justice that he should exercise police powers);[1] and there is even more than a hint again that a girl who drowned herself may have been attempting to imitate a young man, a near neighbour, who had been killed, a few months previously, beyond the old frontiers. Suicides sometimes come in sudden spurts, and at the same spots, the candidate to suicide is in his or her way as much a conformist as the shopgirl or the apprentice who, in order to establish a tentative relationship, will make the most of such opportunities for unremarked encounter as are offered by public holidays, *fêtes*, ostentatious funerals, Sunday devotions, or the moment when the gates close at the entrance to the public gardens of the Tuileries or the Luxembourg.[2]

Those who do not choose the river tend to favour the relative discretion of the Bois de Boulogne, or the shrubberies off the Champs-

---

[1] In addition to the already enormous burden placed on him in the interests of civil harmony and conciliation among the living and order among the dead. See, on this subject, the bitter complaints of Lefrançois, *juge de paix* of the Section de Brutus, in Germinal Year IV, quoted in my *Reactions to the French Revolution*, p. 275 (B).

[2] '... alons au Luxembourg; nous causerons-là plus à notre aise que dans la rue, & nous n'y serons pas rencontrés le matin . . .' (Restif, *Les Jolies-Femmes*, I).

'. . . On partit, & on fut au *Pré-saintgervais*, qui, vu la saison, était une promenade enchantée; car on sait que le *Pré-saintgervais* n'est qu'un vaste jardin-verger, rempli de fontaines, d'arbres, d'arbrisseaux, & dont les sites sont infiniment variés . . .' (ibid.).

'. . . le jeudi suivant était fête. Je me remis sur la porte, comme le dimanche, & je m'occupai à lire. C'était sur les 5 heures du soir, & il fesait grand jour . . . Je lisais fort attentivement, quand je sentis tomber un papier sur mon tablier de taffetas-noir. Je l'aperçus facilement . . .' (ibid., V). A book constituted an excellent alibi even if one could not read it!

'. . . Il avait obtenu du Concierge du *Jardin-du-Roi*, son ami, la clef du *Labyrinthe*: (on sait qu'il y eut un temps où ce Labyrinthe était fermé, on n'y entrait que par connaissance; sans doute que c'était dans ce temps-là si favorable aux petites parties); & il fit dresser les tables dans cet endroit charmant . . .' (ibid., VI).

Elysées, as if to save the unknown passer-by the spectacle of violent death.[1] Those who throw themselves from high windows or who shoot themselves in locked rooms will take the precaution of doing so away from their normal addresses, troubling to move the breadth of two or three streets, as if in deference to neighbourhood opinion. *On se suicide comme les autres.* Only a young painter, a pupil of David's, a romantic before his time, would have the quirky individuality to throw himself from one of the towers of Notre-Dame;[2] and, as we have seen, there is nothing more drearily predictable than the geography of riverside drownings, save that, further downstream—and very occasionally, upstream—of riverside *repêchages.*

Addresses reveal that 75% of suicides by drowning were of people who lived within a few minutes' walking distance of the river, and many of them in sight of it, making suicide as easy as going on an errand, looking in for a midday glass *chez le limonadier,* or making an everyday purchase. *On se suicide de près plutôt que de loin,* and such accessibility has the appearance of banalising suicide, reducing it almost to the familiar proportions of daily activities. No doubt most of those who killed themselves in the river had witnessed one or more such events.

Suicide rates go up because they go up, as though the word had gone out not only in the brightly coloured, visible world of river, bridge, quayside,[3] and *abreuvoir* where everything is *seen* and reported almost

---

[1] '. . . s'est suicidé led. jour heure de midi dans les Champs-Elysées en se brûlant la cervelle . . . absent de son domicile . . . vers 9 heures et ½ du matin . . . C. *Pierre-Desplans,* employé gardien du muséum central des arts, y demeurant (Muséum) natif de Saint-Nicolas-de-Vérost (Mont-Blanc), 47 ans, marié . . .' (procès-verbal du 4 floréal an IX).

'. . . cadavre repêché . . . dans un trou plein d'eau à l'entrée du Bois de Boulogne . . . C. *François Lanisier,* 64 ans, homme de rivière dit *Bout à port,* demeurant à Grenelle, barrière du Port de l'eau, 66, natif de Paris . . .' (procès-verbal du 30 thermidor an VIII).

There were three further suicides off the Champs-Elysées (Monday, 9 March 1799; Friday, 21 August 1801; Friday, 20 May 1803), one in the Bois de Boulogne (Saturday, 12 March 1803); one *dans le parc de Mousseau* (Monceau?) (Saturday, 7 August 1802); one *au Batignol,* commune de Clichy (Friday, 14 October 1802) and one 'on a bench' in the rue d'Orléans (19 October 1802).

[2] There was a repeat on Saturday, 16 April 1803, when Gulliaume-François Leblanc, *ancien marchand de vin,* 48, threw himself from one of the towers (D4 U1 31).

[3] '. . . Je n'ose presque vous dire la honte de son choix—mais c'était un Re-cruteur du *Quai-de-la-Ferraille.* Vous savez qu'il n'y a que des Malheureuses, des Filles-perdues, qui osent parler à ces Gens-là. . . . on n'entendit rien jusqu'au moment où une voisine d'à-côté, ayant eu affaire au Quai de Gêvres, elle prit en y

as soon as done (and no sooner magnified and multiplied by popular report), early morning, midday, and at dusk, but throughout hundreds of the adjoining boxes formed by *chambres garnies*, jumping a lodging-house here and there, or even scaling a street, but still sticking to the same levels of fourth, fifth, and sixth floor, as though this or that suicide-to-be had taken his or her ultimate decision *d'en finir* after having looked across the street, and penetrated deep into the darkened interior of a room equally comfortless and as sparsely furnished, *en face*, the scene of a recent shooting, hanging, or self-defenestration, in this deep and narrow world of facing windows, only occasionally concealed by long green blinds during the heat of the summer day.[1] Even a man who shoots himself behind a locked door is discovered, a few seconds too late, by his 24-year-old son, by the owner of the house, and by half a dozen *voisins de palier*,[2] as though his intended action, even its time and place—for there would be no doubt about the *manner*, the possession of a pistol being known to a whole household, a whole staircase, as an object too large to hide—had been known in advance. Perhaps, in the ready and enforced sociability of the staircase, he may himself even have talked about it.

How very far indeed are we then removed from *les Mystères de Paris*, a nineteenth-century fantasy, in this so predictable, almost normal, geography, calendar, and familiarity of eighteenth-century

---

allant celui de la Ferraille. . . . & y vit Honorée, en conversation avec son Amant . . . elle se promit seulement de dire à sa Jeune-voisine qu'elle s'exposait, en parlant à ces sortes de Gens sur le quai. Mais à son retour, quel fut son étonnement . . . de retrouver encore Honorée au même endroit, causant avec le Recruteur! . . . tout le Quartier pouvait la reconnaître . . .' (Restif, *Les Jolies-Femmes*, VIII). See also: '. . . Un soir que j'étais assise au frais à la porte de la boutique de ma Sœur, écoutant chanter cet Homme que le Peuple appelle le *Beau-Chanteur*, & qui a choisis le *Quai-de-la-Ferraille* pour donner son concert journalier, un grand Jeune-Homme s'approcha de moi par derrière, & me dit . . . Je me retournai & je vis un Jeune-officier, que je pris d'abord pour un Recruteur. Je ne me gênai pas, le croyant un Voisin . . .' (ibid.).

[1] '. . . Sur le derrière, au même étage, il y en avait deux autres [pièces] plus petites . . . un jour de Quillebrune, en rentrant chez lui, vit une jeune et jolie Personne appuyée sur la fenêtre de l'escalier . . .' (op. cit., X). See also: 'Pourquoi êtes-vous là à la fenêtre, Mlle?—Maman, j'ai senti que j'avais besoin d'air—Babet, mettez les accoudoirs, puisque Mlle aime l'air, elle va le prendre à côté de moi . . .' (op. cit., IX). The mother is no fool; if Babet is going to look out of the window, she will have to do so beside her!

[2] '. . . *André Sauvé* est décédé le jour d'hier vers les 6 heures du matin dans une chambre au 6ᵐᵉ . . . qu'il s'est brûlé la cervelle . . . qu'il s'étoit enfermé au verrou, que la propriétaire et les voisins sont montés et l'ont vu mort, un fils de 24 ans étoit présent . . .' (greffier du juge de paix de la Division des Halles, 29 mars 1798).

Parisian self-destruction and sudden death: an act indeed of such familiarity that it might be seen merely as a speeding-up of a popular *film-à-épisodes*, in pictorial squares, depicting the stages in the life of a man or a girl who goes astray at some early stage: an unwanted pregnancy, a dishonour to the family—always the relentless pressure of *honneur, honneur, honneur*,[1] something so infinitely precious, even more so than lace cuffs and *mirṣas*—a minor theft from a workmate or from a sleeping-partner, drink, dice, cards, billiards, a brawl, a *saisie*, a change of address,[2] a removal at night, through the window,[3] the *commissaire de police* (who, of course, knows *all*), Saint-Lazare, Sainte-Pélagie, the Force, then in the last square: out of the window, the noose, the chair kicked away, the pistol in the mouth, over the bridge (in *enjambement* position), to be drawn out with a pointer, and commented on in the iron voice of the fairground; the Saturday-night fight or fall downstairs, all six storeys, or over the banisters ('it was *your* round and you did not pay for it'); the Sunday-morning suicide favoured by girls; the Monday-morning suicide favoured by young men; the mid-week or *any* day suicide of the very old with time on their hands, and too impatient even to reach the end of a week rendered intolerable by pain and hopelessness. Again, if April–May (Floréal) is the great marriage season, after Lent, it is no doubt also that of broken promises, lost hopes, and of sudden masculine absences, so that it also becomes that of female suicide, such is the close association between expectation shattered and self-destruction.

Men are either sooner in the river, as if in response to the military killing season, or they are lagging behind the women and girls, to-

---

[1] '. . . Ils nous firent passer pour tenir au mauvais commerce publiq. Ils assurèrent qu'on recevait chez nous tous les Hommes qui se présentaient. Ils feignirent d'y venir, entrant mystérieusement dans l'allée, d'où ils sortaient successivement après un séjour de quelques minutes, & affectant de dire à la porte *Il y a presse: Il faut attendre son tour pour ces Déesses-là!* Le Curé fut scandalisé de tout ce qu'il entendait sur notre compte: une foule de gens certifiaient qu'on voyait journellement entrer & sortir des libertins de chez nous . . .' (Restif, *Les Jolies-Femmes*).

A husband, whose wife had disgraced him by her public misconduct, making him an object of ridicule, 'quitta le quartier-marchand où il demeurait, pour aller dans une rue plus tranquille, où il se mit *par haut*, ne voulant plus faire son commerce en boutique' (ibid.). 'Avoir pignon sur rue' could thus be a dangerous form of exposure to public observance and comment.

[2] See my *Sense of Place*, the section on Lyon. See also Restif, *Les Jolies-Femmes*, '. . . le soir, malgré la sévérité de la Police, il y eut un petit charivari. C'est une chose cruelle pour un Homme délicat! Un Assassin fait quelquefois moins de mal qu'un Rieur qui donne le charivari!—l'Epoux cependant gardait le silence; mais il usa de l'avantage que donne Paris, il changea de demeure . . .'

[3] See my *Police and the People*, p. 265.

wards the end of summer, and towards the conclusion of the revolutionary year. All Souls' Day, which, in this six-year cycle, falls on
either 11 or 12 Brumaire, is devoid of any suicide, though there are a
couple on All Saints' Day. There is one girl who hangs herself on
Christmas Day.

Sunday suicide by girls suggests a connecting link between suicide
and leisure. Sometimes the link seems to have been the simple one of
time: the time taken to reach the river from addresses that were as
much as or more than an hour's walk from the Seine. A further link
may be observed between *la promenade du dimanche*, the Sunday walk
in company (another girl, or two men and another girl, there is safety
in numbers; but numbers also accelerate conversation and favour
mutual seduction) to the banks of Chaillot, Passy, and Neuilly, followed, on another Sunday, in spring or early summer, by the same walk
alone, the girl drowning herself at *le Point du Jour* (a sad irony), *Au
Moulin Joli*, 'en bas de Meudon', or opposite l'Ile des Cygnes.

As we have seen, accidental drowning offers even fewer areas of
mystery and speculation. The 9- and 10-year-old boys, their elder
brothers, cousins, or neighbours of 12, 13, and 14 head for the quayside
in droves at dusk, in July and August, fellow apprentices in the same
workshops, and enlarge, to fit the length of the banks of the midsummer
river, the range of acquaintances among their contemporaries so as to
include even boys from the opposite bank—a distant, remote territory.
At periods of extreme heat, even faraway inland Divisions on the
northern and southern fringes of the city would empty their juvenile
and adolescent male population down the whole length of the rues
Saint-Martin and Saint-Denis, and Saint-Jacques, and the land-locked
stinking and stuffy Temple and Gravilliers, extending the ready sociability of anonymity and nudity or semi-nudity to include older and
possibly less innocent *fervents* of the river: medical students, soldiers,
sailors,[1] schoolboys, as well as those who come to the river to water
their horses and those who come there to steal the clothes of the swimmers (the *fripiers* being most conveniently located in alley-ways leading
off the quai de la Mégisserie). Once in the dangerous river, the evi-
dences of trade, occupation, status are left behind on the bank, in
multicoloured piles of striped, checked, or uniform garments, the
bather carrying with him only the distinguishing marks of a personal
geography, with perhaps at most a large handkerchief to cover the

[1] 25 thermidor an X, *Gilbert Dillay*, 'natif de Paris, 22 ans, ex-marin, de présent
cordonnier, dt. rue de Malte . . . absent depuis le 23 . . . cadavre nu repêché le
24 . . .' (D4 U1 31).

private parts or a red cotton square (*madras*) tied turban-like around the head to protect the hair, and giving to the native-born Parisian boy an air of exoticism, as if he had recently escaped from the slave ship of the Barbary pirates.

The discarded clothing, if not stolen, will be recovered by companions in work and in leisure, some of it will eventually reach the Basse-Geôle, several days or weeks ahead of the naked body, and it will go on for many years beyond the brief lives of these drowned boys, adolescents, and young men: 1789–1799, 1789–1796, 1793–1800, 1794–1801, 1780–1795, 1776–1797. What awareness, one wonders, had these dead and, till 1795, schoolless, boys of the realities of the revolutionary period? What indeed would the Revolution have spelled out to the 9-year-old son of a chimney-sweep living in the Gravilliers? Did they even think of relating their truncated boyhood to the visible calendar of revolutionary violence, their lives appearing as little more than abbreviated textbooks, crammers' aids to a short cut through the argumentative tangle of revolutionary history? Had they lived, their expectations would have been entirely predictable: *décrotteur, savetier, porteur d'eau, ramoneur, commissionnaire, gagne-denier*, lives that would have scarcely impinged at all on public, chronicled history.

Other areas of accidental death are equally lacking in mystery. Women were much less exposed to work accidents than men, because they did not work at heights,[1] were not engaged in river transport,[2] were not employed as carriers or unloaders on the ports, were not in the habit either of fishing or urinating in the Seine,[3] and were marginally less likely to fall into the river when drunk. Of course

---

[1] '. . . que le cadavre masculin gisant sur le pavé d'une maison sise rue de la Monnaie No 8 . . . lequel s'est tué en tombant de la toiture accidentellement étant occupé comme garçon couvreur à dresser une échelle de 12 pieds le long du lambrisé de la toiture. . . . C. *Charles-Sulpice Trousseau*, . . . 23 ans, natif de Paris, rue Bordet, 6 . . .' (procès-verbal du 17 nivôse an IX).

'. . . noyé accidentellement . . . en travaillant au quai Dessaix. *Nicolas Leroy*, journalier, 34 ans, natif de la Brosse (S-et-O), sans domicile connu . . . noyé accidentellement en travaillant à la construction du quai Dessaix près le Pont-au-Change. *Jean-Nicolas Oducoeur*, journalier, 39 ans, natif de la Brosse (S-et-O), sans domicile connu . . .' (procès-verbaux du 18 vendémiaire an IX). The two men, much of an age, came from the same village in the Ile-de-France.

[2] '. . . noyé accidentellement aux Invalides . . . *Jean Porrot*, journalier, travaillant au bain, au bas du tertre du Pont-Neuf, et y demeurant, natif de Budling . . . (Moselle), non-marié . . . 44 ans . . .' (procès-verbal du 12 germinal an IX).

[3] '. . . noyé accidentellement en passant l'eau le 15 nivôse dernier [a Monday] C. *Alexandre Brigandin*, journalier, natif de Soisy-sous-Etiolle (S-et-O), demeurant à Châtillon-sur-Orge, commune de Véry (S-et-O).' He fell in the river at Conflans-Charenton (procès-verbal du 3 ventôse an IX).

houses, when they collapsed in the street, on to whoever happened to
be passing, did not distinguish between the sexes; and poor *women*,
being more often engaged than men, in fetching and carrying, in going
from one end of the city to another, delivering laundry or carrying un-
finished articles of new or repaired clothing, were, like small children
sent out on errands, more exposed to the danger of being run over.[1] On
the other hand, if death in childbirth hardly figures at all in the *procès-
verbaux*—half a dozen cases, all for the Year III—it was because this
was not the sort of sudden death to come the way of the two *concierges* of the Basse-Geôle. It is the bodies of *men* that are revealed as
having bandages around their middle, a further reminder of the armies
of those who gained a summary livelihood, before inevitable incapaci-
tation, by carrying immense weights; the function of such bandages
occasionally described as tied around women is not so easy to discover,
women, in eighteenth-century conditions, being more likely to carry
weighty objects on their heads than on their backs.

All this is fairly obvious. Sudden spurts of consecutive suicides are
less so, unless, as we have suggested, they may have carried their own
form of persuasion: March 1796, February–March 1797, January–
February 1798, April 1798, July–August 1798, March–April 1799,
October 1799, April–May 1800, November 1800, and April 1801. The
pattern is at least consistent as illustrating the annual crop of spring
suicides by drowning, though 1799 and 1800 demonstrate in addition a
most unusual concentration in October and November.

In a society so closely knit and so necessarily gregarious as that of
late-eighteenth-century Paris, one feels that there was a time and a
place for everything: for dying, for being born, for courting, for getting
married, for going to the fair, for getting drunk, for quarrelling, for
wife-beating, for picking pockets; and that this calendar, dating back
many years before the Revolution, owed nothing to the revolutionary
period, indeed ignored it altogether.

In an almanac published in Antwerp in 1816,[2] the Revolution and

---

[1] '. . . cadavre féminin . . . écrasé à mort par une voiture publique dite vul-
gairement fiacre. . . . Citoyenne *Marie-Nicole Poirée*, femme de Pierre-Guillaume
Tiercelin, marchande revendeuse, native de Paris . . . 53 ans . . .' (procès-verbal du
22 nivôse an IX).

[2] *Almanach d'Anvers pour l'année 1816* (à Anvers, chez Jacques Mesne). In an
abrégé chronologique, depuis 1789 jusqu'en 1815, the almanac displays a firm sense
of local relevance: '. . . 1810. Le 9 novembre, arrivée à Paris des 6 premiers
bateaux, venant du canal de Saint-Quentin . . .
. . . 1812. Le 28 janvier, inondation des houillières de Beaujonc, près de Liége
. . .'

even the not so distant Waterloo disappear without a trace, like scum
on the surface of a still pond when exposed to the bright rays of the
sun; and we are left with a much older, traditional calendar of popular
Walloon and Flemish saints, of Habsburg weddings, of the great fairs
of the old Austrian Netherlands, together with those of Lille, Valenciennes, Maastricht, and Cologne, as well as well-tried cures for all the
commonest ailments, including snake-bite, dog-bite, hernia, and blood
pressure. Suicide, too, as we have seen in the case of a rival almanac,
that of Liége, was something that could likewise qualify for inclusion
in such a summum of popular wisdom and—no irony intended—of
human continuity—provided that it could be dragooned into offering
some moral lesson such as the dangers of gambling, the burden of debt,
the naïveté of girls, the implacable weight of guilt; though it would
have been a pity if Denelle *had* succeeded in his attempt on his own
life, once he had killed most of his family, for then he would have
cheated the *bourreau* and the general public of his exemplary appearance
on the Place de Grève in July 1795.[1] What, in fact, the Liége calendar
and the *Messager Boîteux* do not suggest in *any* way, apart from giving
the information that he had been a member of a Revolutionary Committee in the Faubourg, was that his terrible crime was not merely a
private act of violence, but that it had political implications. Suicide
had to be drilled into illustrating a private popular morality. At this
level, it was not to be allowed a political significance.

Nor is the calendar of the nine murders listed particularly helpful,
save to suggest that murder was a very rare phenomenon,[2] and what
might have been guessed in any case: that murders tend to take place
on Friday and Sunday evenings or in the course of Sunday-to-Monday
night (there are four Sunday murders, two Friday murders, two Thursday ones, and one on Wednesday). The body of a 14-year-old boy,
'environ 4 pieds, une contusion à la tête paraissant provenir d'un
instrument tranchant, vêtu d'une mauvaise veste . . . ayant aux mains
d'anciennes marques de brûlures' is recovered from the river at Passy at
the end of October 1795. On 30 December of the same year, the body
of a girl, stabbed to death in her bed, is discovered at 175 rue des Poulies. A new-born baby turns up in the river Bièvre in April 1796; and,
in October of the same year, the corpse of a murdered officer (we will
return to this case) is recovered from the river near Chaillot. In July
1797, a *fille de confiance*, aged 29, is discovered assassinated in the apart-

[1] See Note F, p. 110.
[2] The records of the *juges de paix* of the twelve *arrondissements* provide only
one other murder during our period. See Note H, p. 112.

ment of her employer in one of the buildings of the Louvre; on this occasion, the murderer appears to have been known (*attendu que le prévenu de cet assassinat n'a pu être arrêté*). On Christmas Eve 1797, the dismembered body of a former *garçon-limonadier* is discovered, the trunk in the rue de la Mortellerie, the head and the arms in the rue du Petit-Musc (the *concierges*, at least on this occasion, refrain from suggesting that he might have done it himself). In October 1798, the body of a 36-year-old chimney-sweep from Savoy, its legs and arms tied together with rope, is brought out of the river and at once identified by two shoemakers living at the same address as the murdered man: no further questions are asked. On a Friday-to-Saturday night of March 1799, a man with a nickname is murdered in a wine-shop situated on the quayside at the level of the Grève. Finally, in September of the same year, the body of a well-dressed Rouennais, temporarily in Paris, and staying with his sister, is discovered near the pont de la Concorde.

Such figures are of course of no statistical value; but they can be supplemented from other sources, particularly from the papers of the Minister of Justice for these years.[1] From these too it emerges that murder had become very unusual in the allegedly anarchical Paris of the Directory. For instance, to take one count, between late December 1797 and mid-July 1800, a period of 30 months, the judicial records for the capital give a total of 34 murders, 9 of the victims being women, 9 attempted murders, and 6 cases of homicide. For the same period, 1,620 persons were convicted of minor thefts, mostly of articles of clothing, 900 of those convicted, over half, being women: at most, then, a dozen or a score a year, for a population of 700,000. Another source reveals a total of 13 murders for ten months of the Year VI, 20 murders for the Year VII, and 6 murders for the Year VIII, that is, 39 murders in 36 months, with a surprising concentration of eleven murders in the single month of Frimaire Year VII (November–December 1798), possibly attributable to a sudden spilling-over into Paris of the activities both of the bande d'Orgères and of some of the north-eastern bandit groups. But most such murders seem to have been confined within the circle of the family: wife-slaying, husband-poisoning, infanticide, others provoked by inter-regimental rivalries, or by quarrels between soldiers and civilians, a few committed without apparent premeditation, in the course of interrupted burglaries in closed premises at night. In all these cases, there had, on the contrary,

[1] A.N. BB 18 739–63 (papiers du Ministre de la Justice, Département de la Seine, an IV–an IX).

been no difficulty in identifying the murderer or the murderess, generally known by name and by sight to a whole quarter; in nearly all, they had been caught within the city, in *garnis*, or while attempting to leave it, on foot or by public transport.

To return to the nine who figure in the present *fonds*, as might be expected there is little to be learnt about the victims, apart from the usual information concerning their names, age, place of birth, occupation, and of course clothing; but there are occasional indications of a savagery so extreme as to suggest an act of vengeance, as well as of a time, a place, and a season that might induce even the most prudent to come out of hiding. Pierre Saint-Saulieu, a 35-year-old Norman, living in a lodging-house near the river, was murdered with extreme and loving brutality, on Christmas Eve, his head and his arms then separated from his body. The remains having been identified by his brother, a grocer living on the Left Bank, the latter was at pains to draw attention to the fact that 'notamment le corps a un signe qu'il porte sur l'épaule droite . . .', a clear suggestion that the murdered man had been branded and sent to the galleys and that, venturing out at the festive season, he had encountered some fellow *ex-galérien* who had no doubt been waiting for such an opportunity for a matter of years. Certainly the macabre details of the crime would suggest a *règlement de comptes* in the most elaborate tradition of criminal vengeance.[1]

The murder of a *lieutenant des vétérans*, a 37-year-old bachelor, presumably an Alsatian—his name is Joseph Rol—on a Saturday night in October 1796, is perhaps of a more general interest than the *grand-guignolesque* discovery of the rue de la Mortellerie and the rue du Petit-Musc over Christmas, at least as an indication of what four soldiers might get up to with their spare time on an evening out while in Paris. Rol had gone to the Champs-Elysées with three companions, all from his regiment, who had last seen him heading off into the shrubbery at about 9 in the evening, presumably in pursuit of a woman; in any case, they did not think of following him, eventually making their way back to their barracks in *la Nouvelle France*. The naked body of their companion was recovered from the river, below Meudon, nine days later. On learning this, the three at once came forward with the suggestion that he had been stabbed to death, had been robbed of his clothes (a uniform, especially if it were complete, was a particularly valuable acquisition, and always much in demand by those who had not the least intention of putting it to its official use) and of the contents of the pockets (as it was a Saturday night they might contain a

[1] See Note I, p. 113.

fair-sized sum), and had then been thrown into the Seine. The stab-wounds behind the head, at the back of the neck, and on the shoulders were still visible when the body was retrieved. His three companions treated the certainty of his murder in a matter-of-fact way, as though it was the most normal thing in the world to have happened to some-one who ventured into the undergrowth of the Champs-Elysées, in the dark, after 9, on a Saturday night in October. The Champs-Elysées was obviously regarded as something of a dangerous jungle by soldiers and others partly acquainted with Paris, as contemporary Lyonnais would have regarded the sinister and dangerous Brotteaux. It was a dramatic but apparently not entirely unexpected end to a Satur-day-night outing which had no doubt started out with promise, the four men hunting in a pack, as one might expect of soldiers. Perhaps the victim, who was the only officer in the party, had more money on him than his companions (a sergeant and two members of the regimental band) or more money anyhow than he would have wanted them to know.[1]

Riton, dit *Cadet*, who was assassinated on a Friday night 'dans la maison du C. Folignier, marchand de vin, Port de la Grève No 11' no doubt hides a somewhat doubtful past under his nickname: perhaps an ex-soldier, perhaps an ex-convict, possibly a horse-dealer. He may have had a chance and unwelcome encounter with someone of his own kind from that past; or he may simply have been killed in a drunken brawl (for the *procès-verbal* does refer to '*les auteurs de cet assassinat*').[2] As the murderer of Elisabeth Desnoux, the 29-year-old *fille de confiance*, was known by name to the authorities, once he had made his escape, he was presumably a lover or a close friend of the girl.[3] But the murder of

---

[1] '. . . *Joseph Rol*, lieutenant au 94ᵐᵉ compagnie des vétérans nationaux . . . cadavre repêché le 20 nud et noyé . . . sur le territoire de Meudon . . . 47 ans . . . célibataire . . . avons remarqué l'empreinte de plusieurs coups à la tête, au derrière du cou et sur les épaules . . . disparu le 11 . . . qu'il étoit encore ce jour-là à 9 heures du soir aux Champs-Elysées, que n'ayant reparu depuis, ils présument qu'il a été assassiné et jetté dans la rivière . . . reconnu par deux musiciens et par un sergent du 94ᵐᵉ compagnie de vétérans' (procès-verbal du 23 vendémiaire an V).

[2] 'Il appert d'un rapport du juge de paix de la division de la Fidélité du 28 ventôse an VII que dans la nuit du 18 au 19 dud. mois de ventôse an VII le C. *Riton* (dit *Cadet*) a été assassiné dans la maison du C. Folignier, marchand de vin port de la Grève No 11, qu'on n'a pu découvrir les auteurs de cet assassin [sic] et que le cadavre a été transporté de suite à la basse-geôle' (procès-verbal en date du 16 frimaire an VIII). We do not know why there was a delay of ten months be-tween the murder and the making out of the report.

[3] '. . . *Elisabeth Desnoux*, 29 ans, native de Boulogne-sur-Mer, fille de confiance

the clerk from Rouen, Jacques Chevreuil, while on a visit to his sister, a laundrywoman, remains entirely mysterious; he was unusually well-dressed, but he cannot have been murdered for his clothes, as they were all on his body. Apart from his sister, his body was recognised by a *rentier* living in the *garni* at which the murdered man had been staying, and which was close by the one from which Saint-Saulieu had set out, two years earlier, before his dismemberment, and by a *conducteur de diligence* employed on the route Paris–Rouen, and no doubt an acquaintance from the latter place: the usual evidence of a provincial network preserved within the city, and revealed by a chance stabbing.[1]

Certainly a selection so random, imposed entirely by the administrative accident of having been scooped up in the wide net of *la mort violente* reserved primarily for the drowned, cannot witness in any useful way to the nature of crimes of violence within the capital. But it does possess a limited negative value. Unlike the *affaire Denelle*, which, whatever the One-Legged Messenger might argue, *was* a political crime (Denelle himself said as much), none of these murders can be said to go beyond the restricted area of *le domaine du privé*. With murder, as with suicide and other forms of sudden death, public history remains firmly excluded from a *fonds* that, only very occasionally—perhaps some of the anonymous suicides of Prairial Year III, the young man killed on the plaine de Grenelle, the two women killed by the bomb of December 1800[2]—reflects, in a humble and tragic manner, the

---

chez la citoyenne veuve Berrieux, Maison Nationale du Muséum, pavillon du Nord . . . avoir été trouvée assassinée dans la maison de ladite veuve . . . attendu que le prévenu de cet assassinat n'a pu être arrêté . . . les administrateurs de la municipalité seront invités de la faire inhumer séparément' (procès-verbal en date du 14–15 messidor an V).

[1] '. . . *Jacques Chevreuil*, commis chez un marchand à Rouen, natif de Bonnet-le-Louvet (Seine-Inférieure), 49 ans, domicilié à Rouen rue aux Juifs, disparu depuis le 7 vendémiaire an VIII, cadavre . . . trouvé près le pont de la Concorde . . . ayant au côté gauche une blessure faite avec un fer pointu qui annonce qu'il a été assassiné, qu'il avoit sur lui une chemise marquée *I.C.H.*, un bonnet de laine marqué *F.A.*, un habit de drap de Sylésie couleur mélangée bleu et blanc, un gilet de drap rouge et brodé à grandes fleurs blanches et vertes, une culotte noire de satin turc, une paire de bas de laine noire, un chapeau de laine à 3 cornes & une paire de souliers à cordon, le cadavre est reconnu par sa sœur, Marie Chevreuil, femme Rairier, blanchisseuse, demeurant à Paris rue S. Marc no 12, par Jacques Chohecq, conducteur de diligence, demeurant à Paris rue des Prouvaires, et par Michel Trépard, rentier, demeurant 363 rue Jean-Jacques Rousseau . . .' (procès-verbal en date du 11 germinal an VIII).

[2] '. . . cadavre féminin tuée le 3 nivôse . . . rue Nicaise . . . à 8 heures 20 minutes par l'explosion . . . *Jeanne-Elisabeth Hugault* . . . de près de 22 ans, native de

course of general history. One can at least understand why murder should not have been one of the principal preoccupations of the judicial and police authorities: it was not really a problem. But, because it was so rare, it could also send shock-waves of horror through a whole quarter. We can be quite sure that the macabre circumstances of the death of Saint-Saulieu—rather a fine name for a *garçon-limonadier*, so fine that one suspects it must have been stolen from somewhere—would be long remembered, and recounted with loving exactness, in the riverside quarter of the rue de la Mortellerie and the rue du Petit-Musc.

Paris, marchande de marée et de fruits, demeurant rue des Vieilles-Etuves No 57 . . . id. *Adélaïde Agnée Norice*, femme divorcée Lislés, sans état, native de Paris, env. 42 ans, rue de Lille 680 . . .' (procès-verbaux des 4 et 5 nivôse an IX).

On 3 Nivôse, the *juge de paix* of the Division du Muséum called to the scene of the explosion, enumerated four more victims: (i) 'un cadavre de sexe féminin, décédée rue Nicaise No 511, chez de Metz, marchand chapelier . . . 3 jupons, un de différens morceaux de toile de Rouen . . . dans les poches, un dé en cuivre, une petite brosse à dents . . . un anneau . . . d'oreille en or . . .'. (ii) 'un autre, de sexe féminin absolument nud, les 2 bras emportés ainsi que la cervelle . . . défiguré au point de ne pouvoir en faire le signalement, attendu que la 1ère peau du visage est totalement emportée . . .'. (iii) 'un cadavre de sexe masculin . . . ayant des bottes aux jambes . . .'. (iv) 'un autre cadavre de sexe féminin . . . un tablier de taffetas noir . . . dans les poches . . . une lettre imprimée d'un bureau de confiance, servant à placer des individus at portant l'adresse de Madame Lystère, rue de Lille [she must then have been a domestic servant who was in search of a new position or who had already found one] . . .' (A.D. Seine D1 U1 35, juge de paix du Muséum).

(iii)

The *répondants* and the network of neighbourhood, work, and leisure

'. . . *Jean Soyer*, nourrisseur de bestiaux, natif de Saint-Front (Orne), 36 ans environ, domicilié à Montrouge, marié . . . une chemise marquée *I.S.*, un gilet de nankin gris rayé jaune, une veste de toile bleue à rayes blanches, une blouse de toile idem . . . cadavre reconnu par Guillaume Soyer, nourrisseur de bestiaux, demeurant à Montrouge, par René Soyer, charetier, demeurant à Paris, rue de l'Oursine, No 26, Division du Finistère, étant les frères du défunt . . .'

Procès-verbal en date du 19 prairial an VIII

'. . . rue de la Ferronnerie, place des carosses (Marchés) . . . un particulier étendu par terre . . . avons appris que ledit particulier étoit cocher de place, que sa voiture étoit sur ladite place . . . que ledit cocher avoit bu un coup et mangé un morceau, & qu'en sortant & arrivé près de sa voiture, il étoit tombé . . . est arrivée la citoyenne veuve Grosclère . . . nous a dit qu'elle est propriétaire du carosse *No 1006*, qu'elle reconnoît parfaitement led. particulier pour être son cocher, qu'elle croit qu'il se nomme *Allart*, qu'elle ignore sa demeure . . . qu'elle a été chez Mercier, loueur de carosses, rue de la Réunion, chez lequel ledit Allart a servi longtems, qu'elle a été chez Fontaine, commissaire de police de la Division de l'Indivisibilité à la Mairie, que toutes les recherches ont été inutiles . . . attendu . . . l'impossibilité de découvrir les parents et amis dud. Allart, disons qu'il sera inhumé par la municipalité du 4ᵐᵉ arrondissement.'

Procès-verbal en date du 27 messidor an VII

'*Sébastienne Victoire Rivoal*, tabletière, en carton, 19 ans, native de Paris, y demeurant, rue du faubourg Martin, No 197 . . . une chemise marquée *R*, une camisole d'indienne brune, un juppon aussi d'indienne fond brun à petites fleurs rouges et blanches, un autre juppon de toile grise, une paire de bas de coton bleu, et une paire de souliers à cordon . . . cadavre reconnu pour être celui de sa fille par Yves Rivoal, porteur-d'eau, rue des Vertus, No 67, division des Gravilliers.'

Procès-verbal en date du 7 brumaire an VIII

I F, however, we remove our gaze from the leading figure in each of these completed biographies, to include those who stand on the threshold, our material acquires a new, perhaps unexpected, historical dimension, in which, with one or two exceptions only, the recently dead are attached, too late to be of any help to them, to the far more numerous living (four *répondants* at least for each body), enriching each drowned child with a small network of family: parents, brothers and sisters, godparents—each pensioner, inhabitant of a charitable institution, poor house, or hospital, with a generation or two of younger relatives: children, nephews and nieces, grandchildren. Even the bachelor who shoots himself or the spinster who throws herself out of a window, can raise up, from beyond the grave, a nephew or a sister-in-law, maybe the other end of the town, as well as workmates, shopkeepers, house-owners, *limonadiers*, portresses, *rentiers*, as if one could follow the recently dead in what had been their daily occupations and frequentations, their repetitive itineraries, and the so apparently reassuring round of a banal existence: lived here, bought bread there, ate here, worked there, drank here, played cards there, took an evening stroll here, sat in the sun there, following them around, looking over their shoulders, eavesdropping on their conversation, sensing their delight in small and simple things—the growing shadow creeping up a yellow wall, the deep green of the plane-trees, the sound of *vielles* played lustily by an Auvergnat pedlar, the striking beauty of a girl emphasised by the neatness of her much-darned clothes—a charm that did not pass the observant attention of that *orfèvre en la matière*, Restif[1]—the slight breeze coming off the river, the steadily mounting cascade of insults just teetering towards the dangerous level dividing the permissible from the impermissible, or just the dull click of dominoes—and thus recreating, without undue effort or invention, the small, intimate personal geography of a few streets, even of a whole quarter. The *procès-verbaux* will indeed provide some of the passports to such lost, semi-secret itineraries, to the entries of alleys, to the dark-green doors leading on to walled gardens, and to the sort of knowledge in the possession certainly of any reasonably observant *garçon-coiffeur*:[2] 'his name is so-and-so', 'he is a rich bookbinder', 'you can

[1] '. . . Ils furent enchantés de la propreté des haillons qui la couvraient: ils étaient déchirés, mais propres tirés à quatre épingles . . .' (Restif, *Les Parisiennes*).

[2] '. . . Il s'informa d'elle à un *Coifeur* qui se trouva de sa connoissance; il aprit de cet homme que sa Divinité se nommait Aurore-Marie . . .' (Restif, *Les Jolies-Femmes*).

find him any evening at such-and-such a café, playing cards',[1] 'he has three daughters, one of them recently married', 'they go to Saint-Nicolas-des-Champs on Sundays'. But they will not take us the whole way, so that we will have to address ourselves further to the *commissaires de police* and to the circulars of the Bureau Central.

Even the drowned soldiers are then afforded the doubtful advantage of posthumous recognition by half a dozen people from their own regiment or their own barracks, in their own rank, below it, or above it, so that a *grenadier* may be vouched for by a *sergent-major*, a *maréchal-des-logis* by a *lieutenant*, a *lieutenant* by a hussar, these being his last companions in life, and the first to notice his failure to return to barracks, or to turn up at a prearranged rendezvous the next day, all participants, though presumably unwilling ones, in an egalitarian army in which differences of rank disappear in the expectation of the common enjoyment of leisure. (Much would depend too on who was, on that Saturday or Sunday evening, in money; and a captain would be as ready to be stood a round by a sergeant, as a sergeant by a corporal. Furthermore, after six or more years of war, military solidarity within a mainly civilian city would have been greatly strengthened, if only as a form of self-assertion and self-defence, for these people did not possess the jealously guarded passports that would give them access to the secret itineraries of convention and habit—their uniforms, on the contrary, witnessed strongly *against* them, a fact of which they were well aware, as may be revealed in much of their reported conversation to those outside the military circle.)[2]

It would of course be hard to escape the collective ties of military life, its *servitudes* so very much more obvious than its rare *grandeurs*, even as a result of suicide; and if the corpse eventually falls to the civilian authorities of the city—a self-demobilisation definitive enough —the uniform will probably go back where it came from. But even a passing visitor to Paris will not depart unnoticed: a military bureaucrat from Rocroy is vouched for by three companions from the same small town, all men of condition, two of them staying in a neighbouring hotel. All had presumably arrived together; and it is clear that two of

---

[1] '. . . j'aurois envie de faire la connaissance de Monsieur son Père. La Fille de Modes m'en indiqua le moyen le plus facile, en m'enseignant le Café où il alloit passer les soirées; je l'y joignis; je fis sa partie de *dames*, ou de domino, & nous fimes bientôt connaissance . . . il me mena chez lui . . .' (*ibid.*, VIII).

[2] Especially, it would seem, sailors, even officers of *la Royale*. '*Ma'm'selle* (lui dit-il) *je suis un Marin un peu grossier; mais j'ai acquis de la gloire, & je suis un parti sortable* . . .' (Restif, *Les Contemporaines*).

them had likewise arranged to return together, having booked their places on the Charleville mail coach, and the *suicidé* even having had his trunk sent on in preparation.[1]

We have already referred to the social immobility so strikingly revealed by the lists of the suicides. But a similar phenomenon soon becomes apparent in terms of residence. Nearly half of the 270-odd people with whom we are concerned, seem to have been living, at the time of death, in lodging-houses; and there are plenty of indications that they had been living, if not in the same *garni*, at least in the same street, for a number of years previously. In one case, it is stated that a man in his late thirties had been a resident of the quarter Saint-Denis for seventeen years. Clearly, far from being a temporary cover for a transient, a *garni* could house a man—and indeed his family—for a lifetime of work and hardship. Judging from such scattered evidence as may be gleaned from such unconsciously revealing material, an *habitant de garni* could be as fixed in his habits as an established householder. A laundress has gone out to the river from a street in which all her relatives, male and female, are engaged with the hot iron. The former Consul-General in Philadelphia can muster a distinguished group of *répondants*, one of them Chappe, the inventor of the sun-telegraph, who, apart from similar professional status, also have in common the fact that they all live either on the quai Voltaire or on streets leading on to it.[2]

[1] '. . . *Jacques Gillet*, ex-lieutenant au 1er bataillon des Ardennes, natif de Rocroy, 27 ans, demeurant ordinairement à Rocroy, et logé à Paris depuis environ 3 mois, 603 rue Helvétius, disparu depuis le 15 de ce mois . . . led. cadavre a été trouvé avec une corde au cou qui lui descendit jusqu' à la ceinture, vêtu d'une chemise dont le col est brodé, une culotte de drap ardoise, sans bas, habit ni soulier . . . cadavre reconnu par Jean-Pierre Kellenter, marchand, demeurant ordinairement à Juliers (Roër), de présent à Paris, logé rue et Maison Clos-Georges... François Janes, employé au Ministère des Finances, 211 rue des Poulies . . . et Victor Huart, ex-fournisseur des armées de la République, demeurant ordinairement à Rocroy, de présent logé à Paris même adresse . . . ajoutent lesd. témoins que led. jour [15 prairial] il avoit donné rendez-vous auxd. C. Kellenter et Huart, en son logement, rue Helvétius, que ces derniers s'y sont rendus à l'heure indiquée, que led. Gillet venoit de sortir et qu'on leur a dit qu'il ne seroit pas longtems, qu'ils l'ont attendu jusqu'à minuit passée et qu'il n'est point reparu, qu'il devoit partir le lendemain matin avec le C. Huart pour retourner à Rocroy, qu'il avait même à cet effet fait transporter son portemanteau chez lesdits . . .' (procès-verbal du 23 prairial an VII).

[2] '. . . *Léon Delauney*, ex-Consul de la République à Philadelphie, natif de Laval, 36 ans, 843 rue du Bacq . . . cadavre reconnu par François Chappe, ingénieur télégraphiste, demeurant 23 quai Voltaire, Jean-Baptiste Morcrette, ancien courrier de cabinet, 843 rue du Bacq, Jean-Marie Tant, arpenteur, 924 rue de l'Université . . .' (procès-verbal du 24 germinal an VI).

Of course, such neighbourhood acquaintances, far from indicating long-established ties of friendship or of daily conventional greetings, could equally have been rapidly formed, in the easy *bonhomie* and familiarity of a population subject to regular renewal, with the arrival of spring, or the return of autumn (the *rentrée*, in its eighteenth-century application, may be taken literally, not educationally), and so do not necessarily indicate long periods of acclimatisation. But the general impression offered by the *procès-verbaux* is not at all that of people recently uprooted, insecure, unassimilated in the vast anonymity of an alien and forbidding capital. Whatever were the much feared *dangers de la ville* harped on by the silly and insensitive physiocratic writers, they do not seem those of passing unnoticed. On the ample, and varied, evidence afforded, it is clear that almost every one of the suicides could have had someone to turn to, at the time of the ultimate crisis. A Danish jeweller from Odense has a Parisian wife, and several colleagues, all from the Pont-Neuf or the Cité,[1] while a German suicide has children in the city.[2] A man with an Italian name, and born in London, has a daughter and a son-in-law in the same quarter.[3]

[1] '. . . C. *Winther* (Mauritz ou Maurice) natif d'Odense en Danemarck . . . d'environ 62 ans, ci-devant jouaillier, marié, demeurant à Paris, quai des Orfèvres No 19, cadavre reconnu par sa femme et par des marchands orfèvres . . .' (procès-verbal du 16 prairial an IX).

[2] '. . . *Dackweiler* (*Paul-Guillaume*) facteur d'instruments de musique, natif d'Ybach, Pays conquis, âgé d'environ 48 ans, veuf et remarié, ayant des enfants, demeurant rue Beaubourg, No 306.' See also: '*Mathieu Fogt*, natif de Fribourg-en-Briscorr [sic] (Allemagne), âgé de 34 ans, cordonnier, demeurant 32 rue Germain-l'Auxerrois chez le C. Gourdelle, logeur . . .' (procès-verbal du 3ᵐᵉ jour complémentaire de l'an VIII). Fogt, on the other hand, does not seem to have had any family. '*Pierre-Charles Opdeweert*, 14 ans, natif de Bruxelles (Dyle), apprenti ferblantier chez le C. Villemort, 116 rue Honoré, demeurant habituellement chez ses père et mère, 596 rue des Ménétriers (Réunion) . . . noyé par événement port Nicolas' is the victim of accidental drowning (procès-verbal du 15 thermidor an VIII).

[3] '*Philippe Coronello*, natif de Londres, ci-devant employé à la Caisse d'Epargne, 32 ans, domicilié 710 rue de Lille (Fontaine de Grenelle) . . . disparu depuis le 21 . . . sans qu'on aye eu de ses nouvelles . . . un pantalon . . . une paire de bas marqués P.C., une redingotte de drap tirant sur le gris et déchirée par les manches, une chemise de toile marquée *P.C.* ou *G.C.* . . . un caleçon marqué en deux endroits *P.C.*, cadavre reconnu par son gendre, employé au département de la marine, et par sa fille . . .' (procès-verbal en date du 24 brumaire an VI).

One of the suicides had married a Belgian girl from Mons, who came to recognise the body: '. . . suicidé en se brûlant la cervelle le 15 . . . C. *Dubois* (*Jacques-Théodore*) homme de loi . . . natif de Saint-Germain-en-Laye (S-et-O), 27 ans, marié à Mons (Jemappes) le 15 nivôse an V, demeurant hôtel des Indes, garni, rue Traversière-Honoré (Butte des Moulins) cadavre reconnu par sa femme . . .' (procès-verbal du 17 floréal an IX). (*contd. over*)

So, many of these suicides, who had no doubt been quite unimportant, or had felt themselves unimportant during their unremarkable lives, now appear, ironically, as the principal figures in a circumscribed group that moves around them, eagerly responding to the required formalities of family obligations, the give-and-take of professional and trade conformism (a tailor does not cheat a tailor, one *perruquier* will help another, a *marchand de vin* will not try out his execrable *vin de Paris* on another *marchand de vin*, a *logeur*, unwilling to show his books to the *police des garnis*, will open them to a fellow *logeur*, one prostitute will not steal from another, there is even a basic sort of solidarity in a trade that has to look to itself for any protection at all from a general hostility from outside, a hostility particularly cruel on the part of those poor girls who still have their public honour officially intact, who are the most threatened into falling into this ultimate and irreversible degradation, eighteenth-century popular *mores* being, in this respect, the very reverse of Christian teaching). The everyday sociability and minimal *politesses* of collective leisure reveal small societies carefully cosseted against the threat of unaccustomed violence, of the sudden explosion of anger, of the crossing of a frontier mutually recognisable as separating what is permissible from what is not (*dépasser la mesure* suggests that such measure did indeed exist, and that it was readily definable), and as carefully subjected to an elaborate, if unspoken table of *Musts* and *Must-nots*, as the equally elaborate apparatus inherited, in the interest of a constantly menaced harmony, in the villages of Western Languedoc, described so brilliantly by Yves Castan.[1]

Those indeed who have sinned against the demands of such *politesses*, of such *honnêtetés*, who have stepped right outside the limits assigned by family, convention, trade, habit, and the rough camaraderie of shared experience and shared leisure, are indeed the suicides themselves, who, by their last terrible act, have brought the fact and the reminder of violence to the previously reassuring circle of extended acquaintanceship. Most *répondants*, when they come and vouch for the corpses laid out for inspection, express perplexity at being thus confronted with the certain evidence of suicide: so-and-so had gone off, at such-and-such a time, without a word, and, what is more, had gone off in the morning, as if to work, so that there had been no hint of anything out of the

contd. See also: '. . . C. Helffer '(*Jacques*), cordonnier, natif de Délemont en Helvétie, environ 51 ans, marié et ayant des enfants, demeurant Grande Rue de Chaillot No 50 . . . (procès-verbal du 4 fructidor an IX).

[1] Yves Castan, *Honnêteté et relations sociales en Languedoc 1715–1780*, Paris, 1974.

ordinary, either in the time of their departure, or in the manner in which they had been dressed on departing.

There is the suggestion, in such statements to the *juge de paix*, that the missing person, now found and identified, had somehow *manqué à ses proches*, and even let them down in the eyes of their neighbours, by taking his or her departure in a manner so casual, denying even death its due pomp and the opportunity for an appropriate display of family grief. Life, just *because* it was so hard, was not something to be discarded lightly, like a frayed coat by a rich man, on some sudden unannounced impulse. And so the *répondants* will often fall back on such convenient escape clauses as: 'he was behaving very oddly over the last fortnight', 'she had been completely out of her mind for several months; she had had several previous tries; but we had not been living together for some time' (and the man who makes this statement about his hanged wife had come to her home, accompanied by another woman, whose presence is not accounted for, and the two discovered her dead, with a rope round her neck),[1] 'he was always complaining about a terrible pain in the chest', 'he had become unsociable, avoiding company, not even recognising his closest friends, neglecting to acknowledge greetings in the street, and missing his usual *partie de dominos* ever since the spring', 'he was so proud, he had become silent and morose, no longer confiding even in his family', 'he had gone out in the morning, at the usual time, without saying anything; we thought that he had gone off to work; and after three days, we reported his absence to the *commissaire de police*'.[2] The *répondants* always of course have the last word; and it is natural that it should be one that will place them in the most favourable light; one would hardly expect them to come out with the admission that matters had long been detestably unhappy in the home.[3]

[1] '. . . commissaire de police de la Division du Muséum . . . chez Boisvin, rue de la Sonnerie No 9, à l'effet de constater la mort violente de son épouse, dont le cadavre a été trouvé pendu à une corde . . . le 15 après-midi: *Armande-Catherine Boisvin*, manouvrière dite Defresne, environ 39 ans, native de Paris, femme d'Adrien Boisvin, employé à la trésorerie nationale . . . il résulte des déclarations recueillies par le commissaire de police . . . que le C. Boisvin étant rentré chez lui avec une autre citoyenne a aperçu le cadavre de son épouse attaché par le col à une corde, que depuis longtems cette femme avait l'esprit aliéné et avait déjà fait des actes de démence . . .' (procès-verbal en date du 15 messidor an IX). Boisvin seems to have taken it pretty calmly. One cannot help thinking that the *autre citoyenne* may have had something to do with the poor woman's decision to hang herself.

[2] See Note J, p. 113.
[3] See Note K, p. 115.

In this repetitive chronicle, the living can speak for the dead. There is only one case—and it is perhaps the saddest story, in its stark simplicity, in the whole pack—in which the dying just manages to get in a last word, before expiring: it is that of a poor woman in her sixties, found dying in the snow, in January 1796, just outside Paris, beyond the barrière de Fontainebleau, who, on being picked up, and carried into the warm guardroom, had just enough strength to explain to the guards that she had been to see her husband in Bicêtre, and that she was attempting to get back to an address somewhere near the porte Saint-Denis—or that is what they thought they heard—before she died, no doubt of cold, misery, and wretchedness.[1]

Only rarely will a *répondant* claim some degree of foreknowledge (it would have been surprising if he or she had, since this would suggest that the survivor had in some important way failed to carry out the duty imposed by an elementary sociability towards a blood relative or one by marriage). A neighbour is able to recall, of a married man with a family, that his last words to him, during what had seemed a purely routine visit while passing that way—which he did every working day, at much the same hour—had been: 'please give your mother a kiss from me;' as she was his godmother, he had not attached any particular significance to the remark, thinking perhaps that he was merely going away for a few days; and would he deliver the message? It was only after his friend's disappearance that it had occurred to him that this had in fact been a message of farewell.[2] There is, however, a Swiss *mar-*

---

[1] '. . . mort d'une femme déposée au poste de la barrière de Fontainebleau trouvée couchée sur la grande route expirante sur la neige . . . âgée d'environ 60 ans . . . un mauvais casaquin rapiécé . . . un mauvais jupon . . . laquelle a déclaré venir de Bicêtre où étoit son mari et qu'elle retournoit du côté de la porte Denis où elle demeuroit, qu'elle n'a pu donner d'autres renseignements étant morte dans le corps de garde en faisant cette déclaration . . .' (procès-verbal en date du 13 ventôse an IV). The guards no doubt reported her words accurately, though it is unlikely that a woman of that age would have subscribed to prevailing fashion by calling the *porte Saint-Denis* the *porte-Denis*. An eloquent and brief commentary on the terrible winter of the Year IV.

[2] '. . . Cadavre repêché au Pont de Sèvres, après avoir séjourné environ 10 jours à l'eau, carte au nom de *Du Bost*, 230, rue de la Tonnellerie, cadavre reconnu par sa femme Claude Leclère et par Guérin, tailleur au No 260 . . . qui a de plus déclaré que led. défunt en sortant de chez lui, il lui dit: *tu embrasseras ta maman pour moi*, ce qui annonce qu'il avoit l'intention de se détruire . . .' (procès-verbal en date du 25 germinal an VI).

Similarly, a restaurant habitué announces he will no longer be eating there: '. . . laquelle nous a dit que led. Loiseau mangeoit chez elle, que le jour d'hier [Monday] 10 heures du matin *il lui a dit qu'il ne mangeroit plus chez elle, qu'il*

chand de vin, from the canton de Fribourg, who reacts with what can only be described as remarkable coolness, and certainly without the least expression of surprise, when confronted with the body of his drowned brother. It is difficult to see how he could have obtained news of his disappearance in the first place, as they were living in lodging-houses at the opposite ends of Paris. Anyhow, the *juge de paix*, as usual, asked no questions, and the Fribourgeois withdrew, saying that he was unable to pay for his brother's burial. Such is the strength of family ties.[1]

When the *répondants* turn up to identify the corpse of a former inmate of Bicêtre or of some similar tomb of collective despair, they feel that there is no call on them to elaborate further, apart, perhaps, from adding the information that the deceased had walked out of the place on such-and-such a day, and that they had been told of this by the authorities, on one of their (no doubt rare) Sunday visits to the institution. Clearly, the mere fact of having been sent to *les Incurables*, or of having been confined to Bicêtre as a pauper would have been widely accepted as sufficient reason to have obtained one's final discharge in this definitive manner. And as such people would have owed their original confinement, if not actually to the initiative of close relatives anxious to have them off their hands because they were too old to work and because they took up precious space—perhaps even a third of a room—that could be put to better use, at least then with their permission, there would have been evident hypocrisy in the expression of any surprise or chagrin at such an outcome.

Religious inhibitions may also have contributed to a sense of embarrassment and shame, and they certainly account for the rarity of female suicide, at least outside the entirely abnormal circumstances of

---

vouloit s'en aller et que sous 2 jours on entendrait parler de lui . . .' (A.D. Seine D10 U1 7, devant le juge de paix de la Fontaine de Grenelle, 2 messidor an VI, Tuesday, 20 June 1798).

[1] '. . . juge de paix de la Division des Invalides . . . un homme de rivière a repêché un cadavre . . . à la mâchoire supérieure duquel il manquait une dent par le devant . . . une chemise de toile presque neuve marquée a la hanche des lettres *C.* et *O.* . . . ayant fait fouiller dans ses poches l'on n'y a rien trouvé qu'une petite clef forée et un rasoir à manche noire sur lequel est le nom *Ody* . . . et le 7 pluviôse . . . s'est présenté . . . le C. François Auxence Ody, marchand de vin demeurant ordinairement en Suisse à Neaulbriez, canton de Fribourg, de présent à Paris où il est logé rue Saint-Antoine No 50 . . . que le C. *Claude-Joseph Ody,* son frère, demeurant rue des Saints-Pères . . . étant disparu depuis le 10 vendémiaire dernier . . . il a reconnu son vêtement . . . &Ca' (procès-verbal en date du 21 nivôse an V).

the famine years. Though the suicide of mothers of families who took with them to a violent death one or more of their children are stated to have been frequent in the Years II, III, and IV, the *procès-verbaux* only cite *one* case of a woman jumping into the Seine accompanied by her 9-year-old daughter.[1] There were only ten female suicides recorded for the Year VI, eight for the Year VII, twelve for the Year VIII, and nineteen in eleven months of the Year IX. Popular prejudices on the subject of self-destruction, particularly among young men and soldiers, may also have been influenced by the seeping down to the level of the working population of an unquestioned military code of honour. Cartouche, Mandrin, and Poulaillier would hardly have *known* the word suicide, and, in the counter-society of bold banditry, it would only have been acceptable as a means of cheating the *bourreau*. Perhaps a limited indulgence might have been stretched at least to include a girl crossed in love, or injured in the only wealth that she possessed, her honour. And it might even have made allowance for popular superstition: to kill oneself after having drawn a death card, was at least understandable, as it represented little more than a sudden jog, in a general direction from which there could have been no possibility of pulling back; one could not defy a card, it was a matter of accepting a destiny so clearly revealed. There might even have been a residual sympathy for the unsuccessful gambler, flushed out in the Palais-Royal, itself only a step from the Seine.

One should not, however, attempt to read too much into hints of reticence on the part of the *répondants*. In cases in which a period of weeks or even months—and, in half a dozen, almost a year—had separated disappearance from recovery, the uncertainty as to the fate of a given person must have been both a cause of anxiety and a matter of considerable personal and economic inconvenience to those who remained. A wife whose husband had suddenly walked out on her could not start divorce proceedings, nor could either her side of the family or that of the missing husband form a *conseil de tutelle* to come to an agreement about the appointment of guardians to children who were minors.[2] Nor could she apply to a *comité de bienfaisance* in order to have her name

---

[1] '. . . *Marie-Geneviève Sueur*, femme de Philippe Hudde, blanchisseuse, native d'Alfort-Charenton, 47 ans, rue de Sèvres (Ouest) disparue depuis le 19 germinal, repêchée le 21 à Neuilly . . . led. cadavre avoit sur lui un vieux jupon, à barres bleues, tout rempiécée . . . une vieille paire de bas de fil gris, un corset bleu avec une pièce rouge et une vieille chemise de toile. . . . *Catherine Hudde*, 9 ans, fille mineure de Marie Sueur, qui avoit sur elle 2 jupons bleu et blanc rempiécés . . . un grand tablier . . .' (procès-verbal du 24 germinal an VI).

[2] See Note L, p. 116.

placed on a list of officially recognised *indigence*: she could not be an *indigente*, even if she was effectively starving, if she still had a husband in work, from whom she was not legally separated, and who might be presumed to come back at any moment. The recognition of a corpse, whether by family or by friends, put the official seal on the termination of an existence. The *suicidé* could now decently be forgotten, as someone who had deliberately removed himself from the circle of family and neighbourhood. There would be an end to it, even if, as we shall see, the line separating possible suicide from possible murder was thin enough at the best of times.

Whatever may have lain behind such reticence or such semi-embarrassed protestations, and whatever the living man or woman had previously suffered before suicide, it would hardly have been from loneliness and isolation, save in a few of the cases of the very old; but most of these, too, if they were very poor, would have been cooped up in the dreadful barracks of public charity, *corridor de Belleville*, and that sort of thing,[1] that is, miles and miles of corridors, in the Invalides, or the number of a long dormitory in Bicêtre or the ill-named Petites-Maisons (since it was in fact one immense one). And so something of the sheer gregariousness of daily existence creeps into the house of death, in the wake of these batallions of *répondants*.[2] It was not merely close relations who might ask one of the *concierges* to turn the body over, so as to see if there were a brown mark on the left hip, suppurating pus on the right shin, or a burn or a wound on some other normally concealed part of the person. Witnesses giving the same address as the *suicidé* will know about the position of a bandage, and how long it has been there; and it is quite as likely that they owe the impressive exactness of the observation to the fact that they have slept either in the same room, or on the same landing, have used the same staircase lavatory, and have thus spied the *disparu* squatting, with his breeches down, off the open and noisy forum of the staircase, as to their having noticed that he walked with an awkward gait, his legs wide apart.

All eighteenth-century observers, whether those like *rentiers* and *rentières*, *concierges* and portresses, *marchands de vin* and *limonadiers* who watch the passing world, like fixed lighthouses, from the vantage-

---

[1] '. . . absent depuis le 17, repêché par un bateau de charbon, au port près le pont de Grammont à la pointe de l'isle Louviers c. *François Daube*, militaire invalide, natif de Belleville (Seine), environ 72 ans, demeurant hôtel national des Invalides, Corridor de Belleville, No 32' (procès-verbal en date du 23 floréal an IX).

[2] See Note M, p. 116.

point of a seated or standing position of immobility, or those who, on the contrary, run errands, or who work habitually at ground-floor level, looking up every now and then from their table, to take in the street scene, can read a great deal into a *walk*: the suggestion of an occupation, the hint of a criminal past, if one leg is seen to drag behind the other, as well as an optimistic insouciance, a brimming, pin-headed arrogance, a long period with the armies, a long period at sea (a certain way of shambling along), or the lifelong habit of deferential submission, *courber l'échine*, or the very contrary, a gait that will not easily brook contradiction, jostling, or being got in the way of,[1] an attitude further emphasised by the carrying of a long stick, not merely a decoration, but ready for use against *les importuns* and the insolent. And those who belong to the stationary group, including the attentive, observant, and gossiping *coiffeur* (who talks to make others talk), who take a downward view of each customer, will likewise have had daily opportunity to follow each transmutation of clothing from one owner to another, or the transformation of the same article of clothing, as it steadily alters in shape, character, purpose, and variety of material, on the same owner.

An attentiveness so constant and so vigilant should not be attributed either to the habit of suspicious and alert hostility and mistrust, as if one lived in a permanent state of war and had all the time to be on the look-out for some open or furtive act of aggression, or for the soft skills of the pickpocket, nor, on the contrary, to an open-hearted friendliness, a social candour, towards one's fellows (fraternity might do as a word on public monuments and as a desirable aspiration thought out *dans le secret des cabinets* by those who had long-matured plans for the re-generation of mankind; but it was a concept altogether too abstract for application to the street), but rather to an awakened curiosity about everything and everybody, a curiosity already very bright-eyed in the chimney-sweep, the little *bouquetière*, the *marchande de falourdes*, and the running and skipping daughter of a *laveur des cendres*. Curiosity began as soon as one could walk; and children were well-known to be the best observers, because they were both sharp and not readily noticed. That was why they were so often employed on errands that were not just a matter of fetching and carrying, but also of watching and finding out, and coming back to report what they had seen. Four-foot was often a better observatory than five-foot-six; and it was almost

[1] '... Ce fut surtout au *Luxembourg* qu'il se donna carrière: il se rengorgeait, se tenait raid, ne se détournait pour personne, au point que peu s'en fallut qu'il ne renversât une Dame-de-condition, qui passait à côté de lui: ce qui manqua de lui attirer des coups-de-canne de la part d'un Officier qui l'accompagnait, & qui traita Le-Riellet de Manant...' (Restif, *Les Jolies-Femmes*, VI).

always a better listening-post. And curiosity would go on throughout adult life, becoming almost obsessive in old age, particularly on the part of the elderly woman sitting out on a chair in the street. For the street was much the best spectacle available; and there was probably much more satisfaction in keeping a very close watch on the hourly and daily habits of one's neighbours, and in collecting, over a period of time, the full range of habitual itineraries followed by them, in the working week and at leisure, so as to be able to distinguish, at first glance, between what was normal, and what was out of the ordinary—a matter as much as anything for mild excitement, rather than for alarm— than in the contrived spectacles laid on by the *saltimbanques*, the street actors, those who performed with trained animals. A curiosity so wide-awake when addressed to the living, could readily extend to the dead.

(iv)

The language of clothing and livery

'. . . un habit de drap maron foncé, un gilet de toile de coton fond blanc, à rayes jaunes, une culotte de drap vert, un caleçon de toile de coton bleu à petites cottes, une paire de souliers à cordons, une chemise de toile blanc avec jabot de mousseline unie, une cravate de mousseline blanche à rayes bleues, un mouchoir de poche de toile blanche, marquée en coton rouge des lettres *L.M.*, une paire de gants, un couteau à manche noire, dont la lame est cassée, un tire-bouchon aussi cassé, une petite clef à cadenas avec une ficelle nouée à l'anneau, 14 centimes en décimes, 2 pièces de 5 centimes, 2 pièces d'un sol chaque, une pièce d'un sol 6 deniers, une paire de boucles d'argent qui étoient aux jarretières, et un lambeau de passeport No 6 indication du département de l'Indre.'

Procès-verbal en date du 7 messidor an VIII

'. . . une chemise marquée *F* en fil bleu et des deux côtés de lad. chemise marquée en couleur de rouille qu'on dit être la marque ordinaire du linge de grand hospice d'humanité . . .'

Procès-verbal en date du 3 prairial an VIII

'. . . une chemise marquée *F.G.*, . . . une redingotte de drap bleu ciel . . . un gillet de drap rouge avec boutons dits à la hussarde . . . une culotte de velours vert foncé, . . . une paire de bottes . . .'

Procès-verbal en date du 4 floréal an VIII

'chemise de toile marquée derrière le col *f 39 et 6*, un chapeau à 3 cornes, une perruque ronde . . .'

Procès-verbal en date du 8 fructidor an VIII

'. . . vêtue d'une camisole lilas rayée très mauvaise, un mauvais jupon blanc, un bas bleu et blanc déchiré, l'autre jambe nue et remplie de mal, des sabots, et un petit bonnet rond.'

Procès-verbal en date du 2 nivôse an IV

'mauvaise veste d'étamine beige, mauvais gilet pareil . . . chaussé d'une galoche à un pied . . .'

Procès-verbal en date du 12 prairial an III

'. . . cadavre masculin d'environ 10 ans, vêtu d'un petit gilet et d'une culotte à pantalon de toile écrue rapiécée avec siamoise rayée différentes couleurs, un gilet de drap vert garni de boutons d'uniforme de différens corps, sans bas ni souliers . . .'

Procès-verbal en date du 14 floréal an IV

'. . . vêtu d'un habit bleu, revers rouges, veste et culotte de tricot blanc, bas de laine couleur ardoise, col noir d'ordonnance . . .'

Procès-verbal du 21 germinal an IV

'. . . grosses lèvres, le visage grêlé, ayant été brulée à la joue droite . . . cheveux noirs et gris . . . vêtue . . . d'une chemise neuve marquée *No 8* . . .'

Procès-verbal en date du 15 germinal an V

'. . . une mauvaise chemise de femme sans marque, un petit portefeuille de maroquin rouge dans lequel étoit renfermé une paire de lunettes . . .'

Procès-verbal du 8 germinal an VI

ONLY rarely is clothing, which will always have been derived from a variety of sources, ranging no doubt, even in this fairly well-rooted urban milieu, from a family wardrobe situated somewhere in Flanders, Artois, Picardy, the Ile de France, or the east, to purchases from *revendeuses*, immediately distinctive, as a livery might have been. As befits the period of the Directory, a régime incoherent, undefinable in national terms, hybrid and fast changing, we are moving in a city the inhabitants of which are clothed in half-shades, going about their double or triple occupations in odd quarters, halves, or thirds of different occupational or institutional uniforms. Perhaps out of sheer force of momentum and of bureaucratic habit—because they had always done it, because it had been handed down from some past wisdom, possibly dating back to the *ancien régime*—the *juge de paix* and his two assistants shown an unflagging zeal in transcribing every article of clothing, lending at least a sort of multicoloured individuality to corpses that often otherwise had little to distinguish them, the one from another, apart from the visible fact of sex, hair that was white, greying, or still abundant and distinctive in colour. The effect is one of a massive litany that goes on and on because it goes on and on.

Certainly clothing would hardly offer any sort of key to the personality or to the occupation of the clothed. It might even confuse the visible frontiers dividing the sexes, giving to a *blanchisseuse*, who could at least be presumed to command a certain range of linen, a man's shirt, or to a *revendeuse* what could still be recognised, despite restitching and re-shaping, as the embroidered waistcoat of a *suisse*. An elderly *rentier*, totally ruined by the collapse of the *assignat*, can be found hanging, in a *garni*, in nothing more than a long night-shirt, its front picked out in elaborate Dieppe lacework, and a wig: in this instance, a case of carrying over one period into another.

Thus the clothing that has survived the dead man or woman will not obligingly write his or her biography for us. But, with luck, it may offer a few hints as to the use at least to which leisure was put. For instance, there must be some significance in the fairly well-established suggestion that, of the women and girls who choose Sunday as the day on which to drown themselves, many should first of all put on what must have been pretty well the whole of their existing wardrobe, filling themselves out with skirt after skirt, bodice after bodice, like a Hungarian peasant girl from the Puszta, as they might previously have dressed for Mass. We thus encounter *suicidées endimanchées* in such allegedly unrighteous years as 1796, 1797, and 1798, dressed up in an amazing assortment, not indeed of great finery, but of enormous volume, thus attired as much for suicide in Floréal, as for death in the river in bleak Pluviôse. Getting dressed, or adding to the dress in which one has slept—and, at this level, few people would ever have completely undressed, undressing being a luxury reserved for the professional classes—represents the last but one act of will of the *suicidable*, and, as such, it contains a message, though just what it was will escape us. Could it be an act of residual deference to religious obligations? Or does it simply mean that many women carried at all times the totality of their wardrobe, as the only sure means of ensuring that no part of it was stolen, either during sleep, or while working?

Of course, there is a little more to go on in such evidence than is offered by the timid messages of those about to drown themselves. Men who are accidentally drowned on Sunday or on Monday are as likely to be wearing their working clothes as on a weekday, so that one comes away with the impression that the carter was inseparable from his leather apron and his leather-padded breeches, that the butcher remained girded, like a high priest of blood, in his red and white striped apron even when he went to the wine-shop, and that the *garçon-perruquier* overdressed even more for leisure than for work, in the no doubt mistaken belief that some girl fresh from the country might take him for a *petit maître*.[1] A drowned girl, bearing on her person a medallion of Christ, and wearing round her neck a silver emblem of the Holy Spirit, in the form of a dove, on a chain, must surely have been a Protestant, or have come of a Protestant family, or have had a Protestant upbringing, though she would have been too old to have benefited from the effects of the Edict of Toleration.[2] And there is a revealing

---

[1] '. . . *Jacques Morel*, perruquier, 36 ans, natif de Beaugency (L-et-Ch.) demeurant à Paris 100 rue du Petit-Pont, retiré le 14 à la pointe du massif du Pont-Neuf . . . *trois* cravates de toile blanche, dont une à bordures rouges et marquées *P.L.* . . . et *deux* gilets, dont un de nankin fond bleu et un autre de flanelle . . .' (procès-verbal du 15 floréal an VII).

[2] '. . . *Jeanne-Geneviève Valiton*, célibataire, ouvrière en tabatière, 35 ans, native de Paris, y demeurante rue du faubourg Martin (Nord), disparue depuis le 5 nivôse, retirée le 6 au quai de l'Ecole . . . une chemise marquée *BGC*, un casaquin de toile de coton rouge et bleue, un corset de laine, un jupon piqué de différentes couleurs, un autre jupon de drap verd, une paire de poches de toile blanche, une paire de bas de philozèle bleu, une paire de souliers à boucles de cuivre dépareillées, un tablier de toile bleue rayée, un bonnet rond uni, un bonnet piqué, un mouchoir de col rouge et blanc, la rozette d'un Saint-Esprit attachée à un cordon de soie noire, dans ses poches un mouchoir à moucher bleu et blanc, un Christ de cuivre, 2 clefs et un couteau . . . reconnu par Claude Valiton, rentier, demeurant 1218

uniform common to all that extensive population of *cochers, couriers de la malle*, postillions, *garçons d'écurie*, and so on, who make their living in daily and nightly association with the ten-thousand-odd horses said to have been employed within the city: leather-seated breeches, several pairs of gaiters,[1] much more rarely, top-boots; a uniform that would pick them out as decisively as their distinctive manner of walking, once separated from their mounts.

On the other hand, there is such a repetitive uniformity about: *mauvais jupon, mauvaise jupe, mauvaise chemise, mauvais mouchoir, mauvais bas, mauvaise culotte, rapiécée, mauvais gilet en différentes couleurs, mauvais casaquin, mauvaise redingote, camisole lilas rayée très mauvaise*, 'le tout très mauvais', as to tell us nothing that we could not already have guessed, namely that most of those who ended up in the Basse-Geôle were desperately poor—which is not to say that poverty drove them to kill themselves, as very few poor people ever did anything of the kind—that the inmates of charitable institutions were by definition destitute, and that poor people were forced to undertake the more dangerous jobs. The fact of poverty and want is further borne out by the abjectly inadequate contents of pockets, the handfuls of *liards*, centimes, and other small coins, the retention of broken objects useless at the time, but that were presumably repairable—unless the retention of a broken knife with an ivory handle, of a broken ear-ring, or half a pair of scissors, represents, on the contrary, some minimal luxury, a tiny step into fantasy, a clinging-on to some episode in the past on the part of the possessor, clearly often at pains to hold on to such apparently useless items—and the *quelques hardes* left behind in furnished [*sic*]

---

rue de Sèvres (Ouest), son oncle, par un tabletier et par une femme de tabletier . . .' (procès-verbal du 21 nivôse an VII).

[1] '. . . *Pierre-François Denis*, natif de Paris, 32 ans, charretier chez le C Leclerc, rue de Clichy, et domicilié à Clignancourt, s'est noyé en face . . . en faisant boire ses chevaux . . . deux paires de guêtres . . .' (procès-verbal du 8 floréal an VI).

'. . . *Pierre Pariselle*, voiturier par terre, 55 ans, natif de Paris, y demeurant rue des Jardins 3 . . . *une ceinture de serge rouge* . . . cadavre reconnu par sa fille, blanchisseuse, rue de Bercy no 8 . . .' (procès-verbal du 11 fructidor an VII).

'. . . *Jean Gastal*, gagne-denier, 22 ans, natif de Champaigne (Cantal), demeurant à Paris rue de la Huchette (Thermes) . . . une chemise non-marquée, une veste de laine grise, un gilet idem, un autre gilet d'indienne de différente couleur, une culotte grise de casimir rayé, un pantalon de coutil noir, une ceinture bleue, une paire de guêtres de toile grise . . .' (procès-verbal du 8 floréal an VII).

'. . . *Pierre-François Caillot*, marchand de journaux, 43 ans, native de Versailles, demeurant à Paris rue du Four-Saint-Germain 132 (Unité) . . . un pantalon de drap bleu, un autre pantalon de drap gris, une paire de guêtres de laine couleur ramoneur . . .' (procès-verbal du 24 pluviôse an VII).

rooms. Nor would one expect an institutional shirt, with a number, from Bicêtre, the Petites-Maisons, or the grand hospice de l'humanité, or the Invalides, to be anything other than of very poor quality, worn thin by a succession of elderly wearers thus dragooned into the pale uniform of a wretchedly exiguous charity, the sad, washed-out blue apparently favoured by French régimes over a period of more than three centuries.

But the monotony of such pathetic litanies is liable all at once to be broken with the description of some article or other of clothing that, even if it has seen better days, is still reminiscent of past luxury and of present timid pretension: a range of silks, some shot and shimmering, elaborate braiding, dulled, but still weighted in skilled craftsmanship, stuffs in complicated colours, immense handkerchiefs in bright, reassuring checks, canary-coloured waistcoats, with horn or moleskin buttons, even a few smart bottle-green *redingotes* with high collars at the back. The ex-Consul, as well as having on his finger a gold ring bearing the enigmatic message: *2 Lafter-haire* (perhaps not enigmatic at all, but merely the attempt of the scribe, the *juge*, one of the *concierges*, or the *greffier*, to come to terms with English), is clothed in his own marked shirt, 'un habit de drap brun avec boutons de poil de chèvre à carreaux, un gilet fond jaune brodé en soie', while a 36-year-old carpenter represents, no doubt intentionally, a symphony in blue: 'veste de drap *bleu*, un gilet de velours de coton *bleu* rayé en lozange, un pantalon de coutil *bleu*', a brilliant blue, not the pale colour of charity.

Even more elegant, a drowned employee found wearing two waistcoats, the under one 'de velours bleu avec paillettes d'or incrustées', the very height of luxury. Nor is one surprised to learn that the Dunkirk ship-owner had a wardrobe of *at least* six shirts marked with his own initials (he was wearing No. 6).[1] Equally, the murdered are sometimes richly clothed, such as the clerk from Rouen, stabbed to death in Paris: 'un habit de drap de Sylésie couleur mélangée bleu et blanc, un gilet de drap rouge et brodé à grandes fleurs blanches et vertes, une culotte noire de satin turc', and he even has a hat—perhaps, like the Alsatian lieutenant, Rol, he has actually been killed for his fine apparel.

Generally speaking, bright colours clothe both the affluent and the very poor alike, in an age which mercifully releases the deprived from

---

[1] '*Pierre Chevalier*, négotiant armateur, 39 ans, natif de Dunkerque, logé à Paris, rue de la Tranquillité, maison des Filles Thomas . . . une chemise à jabeau [*sic*], marquée *P.C. Numéro* 6, un gilet de futaine, un autre . . . de piqué . . . un soulier à cordon . . . le cadavre reconnu par un rentier et par un négotiant de Dunkerque, tous deux logés maison de Boston, rue Vivienne, mais demeurant ordinairement à Dunkerque . . .' (procès-verbal en date du 16 brumaire an VIII).

the additional wretchedness of having to be clothed in the sad colours of the *demi-teintes*, like those of a retired servant of 67 discreet even in suicide: '. . . une cravate de mousseline *blanche*, une redingotte de drap *gris*, un gilet de nankin rayé, une culotte satin turc *noir*, et une paire de bas de laine à cottes, *couleur gris de fer*', as if he had dressed himself up funereally for his own funeral. Happily, he is the exception, the elderly being generally as colourful as the young.

The quest would have been much easier before 1789, with a full range of liveries to guide both the police and the historian, an army of dead *larbins* leading both straight to their masters. But, in 1796 or 1798, we are denied such simple signposts, the Directory, a period 'in between' in so many senses, being one that is both beyond and before such conveniently visible signs of servitude, though liveries were no doubt creeping back by the summer of 1801. In any case, such ready identification would hardly have been helpful, owing to the almost complete absence, already noted, of *la valetaille et la piétaille* in the dismal armies of suicide, those engaged in service being represented only by a score of *hommes de confiance* and *filles de confiance*, mostly fairly advanced in age. An elderly *fille de confiance* would be in a position far more vulnerable than that of the general range of domestic servants, who might command a considerable mobility in a period like the Directory, when, in Paris at least, there would be a great deal of new money about. Perhaps it was the knowledge that their masters and mistresses did not themselves have long to live, and that, once they had gone, they themselves would have no one to turn to—and Bicêtre and les Petites-Maisons would appear even more unbearable after twenty or thirty years in the comfort of a good house—even if, as most did, they had nephews and nieces living in the city—that drove these hopeless and weary people to drown themselves.

So liveries and those who had worn them elude us. Perhaps the wearers had merely changed their disguise, as, previously, they had so readily exchanged their liveries; or perhaps, like the former monk who had become a pastry-cook,[1] they had profited from the circumstances of Revolution and war, to change both uniform and occupation. However, in the absence of the precisely varied distinguishing marks offered by the swift-changing braids and brocades of a livery, the previous six or seven years had compensated with another, originally less variegated, form of distinctive masculine clothing. As the war years

---

[1] '. . . *Jean-Louis Melant*, né le 21 juillet 1761 . . . ex-frère Cordelier, exerçant le métier de pâtissier, demeurant rue de la Grande Friperie, 406 . . . repêché en bas de Chaillot . . .' (procès-verbal du 27 messidor an IV).

dragged on, and as more and more people were dragged in their wake into the armies of the Republic, and their extensive fringes, and as many more deserted from the armies and their fringes, *la défroque militaire*—a good phrase for a counter-institution—losing *en cours de route* both lustre and uniformity, and bearing still the visible rents and gashes of the battlefield, or even of some private encounter, and witnessing thus to previous deaths, in a variety of circumstances and places, extends further and further westwards, in the quadruple paths of desertion, peculation, theft, and banditry, eventually partially to clothe those sections of the population that, even after five or six years of war, had managed still to remain well out of reach of the armies.[1] It was probably one of the few advantages of war and conquest to have redounded to the male urban population as a whole. It was also a manner of putting war and its garish accoutrements in their right place. Brass or pewter buttons bearing the engraved words *République Française* were certainly better employed on the jacket or the waistcoat of a 9-year-old boy, or on the embroidered bodice of a laundress, than on the tunic of a real grenadier or a false one: the boy would have been proud of his baubles, the *blanchisseuse* would have emphasised the contours of her bust with such a range of glitter brought out by a red velvet background.

There appears indeed in this ability to put anything that comes to hand to immediate personal and practical use a rather impudent popular commentary on the mutability of institutions, and on the very relative importance of public events. Such durable metal buttons, a dull yellow or a pale silver, used either for their proper purpose, to fasten a jacket or a bodice (the top button left provokingly undone), or merely as objects of display, like a couple of eyes looking backwards, to give the impression that the proud wearer could see in both directions, or like brass or silver shoe-buckles worn on some other part of the body, furnish about the only reminder to the almost entirely apolitical population of the Basse-Geôle that a Republic, of sorts, and still nominally French (extensively so), was still officially in existence, not only in 1797, but indeed in 1801.

Buttons, being exceedingly durable, and so objects of some considerable value among the small treasures of the poor and the toys of chimney-sweeps and tailors' apprentices, must indeed even have sur-

---

[1] '. . . observant qu'il y a env. 4 décades la citoyenne Marie Anne Charpentier lui avoit proposé d'acheter 2 chemises, *dont l'une pour hommes marquée à la République*, l'autre pour femme . . .' (par devant le juge de paix du Nord, 15 ventôse an IV, A.D. Seine D5 U1 25).

vived the official existence of an increasingly anaemic First Republic, and no doubt that of the Empire as well. *Cloth* buttons, made out of cheap material, and better suited no doubt to the austerity of the Year II, when they were first put into circulation, and to the beggarly conditions of the Year III, would have been far more representative of the short span of life normally granted to a French Republic; but, being inferior, easily frayed, and not much to look at, not even reflecting the rays of the bright summer suns of 1795 and 1796, of 1800 and of 1801, they seem to have been little in demand, save to fill in the many gaps left between the rare odd metal button—few could have afforded the luxury of a complete set of these, a sort of provocation that would soon have resulted in the removal of some of them during the night— in the rapid turnover furnished by the wardrobes of *la revente*, a trade that flourished on both political and natural disaster, expanding to the measure of the monthly and annual figures of the military dead, in battle and in hospital, and retracting only in periods of prolonged peace.[1]

It was not just *buttons* that thus worked their way back from Saving the Republic, or from foisting it upon others. The random scattering of the tatters of military uniforms, republican, royal, imperial, as well as imperial *and* royal, the fringes and shoulder-straps of rank, gold thread, black or silver braid, the heavily embroidered frogs of dragoon and hussar jackets, the militarisation of the rag trade, with the blue tunics and the high red collars of what had been the National Guard, now disbanded, all thus contributed to the stiffening and strengthening of the clothing of working men and women, most of them quite indifferent to the hierarchical significance of the remnants of uniforms thus put to unheroic and unexpected everyday service. Drowned girls whose bodies were recovered barely clothed in men's military shirts bearing institutional laundry-marks (*R.F.*, *xxvime lég.*, *32me ligne*, and suchlike), and converted to use, first as chemises, and, ultimately, as shrouds, had had no more thought for French military prestige than would have had an inhabitant of les Petites-Maisons or Bicêtre for the dreadful republican institutions from which they had fled to the river, still wearing such rough institutional clothing as they had been granted by the parsimonious charity of a bitterly divided Republic.

For so many poor people, including children, wearing fragments of what could still be recognised by the discerning eye of the skilled seamstress as military clothing, as it had been transformed at the end of a very long chain of death, desertion, escape, theft, *revente*, unstitching,

---

[1] See Note N, p. 117.

re-stitching, the only significance in such enrichment of the variety of popular tailoring would be that, in the previous years, there had been a great many soldiers about, either stripped in one go, on a scheduled battlefield, or as the result of an encounter with an armed group of bandits or *chauffeurs*, or with such marauders as may have divested the unfortunate Rol, or themselves steadily divesting themselves of one article after another of *l'habillement militaire*, along a chain of inns and wine-shops running from suburbs of towns in the Rhineland and the *Pays Réunis*—Cologne, Dordrecht, Maastricht, Brussels, Ghent, Bruges, Lille, Amiens, Péronne, to the outskirts of the capital: Saint-Ouen, Clignancourt, la Chapelle, on the northern side (though there might still be some coming in also from the west to Gentilly, Arcueil, and Montrouge; Meudon, Sèvres, and Boulogne)—a pair of long boots sold here, leather breeches there, a *bonnet de police* disposed of later, a jacket and a shirt the last to go. Higher up in society, during the Directory, and even more during the Consulate and Empire, the trends of fashion often indicate a servile imitation of military tailoring, with young men prominent in the cowardly ranks of the class 'armies' of the *jeunesse dorée*, who have absolutely no intention of risking themselves on any battlefield farther away than the Palais-Royal, affecting high military collars *à la hussarde* and tightly buttoned topcoats, and even with girls of the newly wealthy adopting hats recalling the shape of a cavalry helmet or Hungarian shako.

But the poor and the very poor were certainly not concerned with such collective manifestations of political conformism and of creeping militarism that, spreading westwards, had begun to infect Paris from the Year III onwards; and their clothing had at no time reflected the passing modes affected by that minority of the population that lived at a disputatious political level: directorial and moderate, neo-jacobin and rancid, anti-republican, vaguely royalist, violent and confused. Even the exigencies of *sans-culotte* fashion, as laid down by such experts as Hébert, Pauline Léon, and Claire Lacombe, while being sedulously followed by small and vociferous groups of middle-class demagogues, seem seldom to have caught on with the politically indifferent mass of the *habitants de garnis*, while the *dames de la Halle* had lost no time in pointing out to interfering actresses that they had no intention of dressing differently from the way in which they had dressed in the past, and which represented above all the manifestation of collective pride, of popular privilege, and of attachment to custom (and to *le bon roi Henri*). Although, in the Year III and during at least the early years of the Directory, efforts were still being made to enforce the regulations about the wearing of cockades, even extending the obligation to men as well as to women, there is not a single instance of a cockade—whether the official tricolor, or the unofficial black, white, or green, denoting various adherences to anti-republican factions—being listed among the clothing of the inmates of the Basse-Geôle. Why should there have been? Cockades were not pretty baubles like brass buttons.

We are engaged in a lost world, in which everything counts, and nothing can be taken completely for granted; the manner of walking, of holding oneself, the angle of a three-cornered hat, the brave show offered by a striped waistcoat, the possession of at least a single-pointed shoe, or of *one* stocking in shot silk, of a pair of brass buttons, the angle of a head, the bold expression of blue eyes, *le regard hardi*. The Basse-Geôle is just beyond the last act of a life flaunted in a series of episodes, carrying, beyond death, the complicated signals of pride, fantasy, superstition, impudence, naïveté, brute strength, dull courage, and low cunning, the message of which may be interpreted by those who know what they spell out.

Clothing, in the unequal importance of its respective items, is thus an affirmation of individuality and variety, of a wealth of choice still available to the poorest, and a rejection of regimentation. The motley armies of the dead are not those of the One and Indivisible; the *suicidés* and the others carry more than the livery of a single occupation in what they stand up in, drown in, and are fished out in. The temporary inhabitants of the Basse-Geôle would have defied the most persistent professional observer: an ultimate victory at least over the forces of repression.

In fact, almost the only style of distinctive clothing that we do *not* encounter, laid out in the hope of eventual recognition, as a sort of posthumous bid for identity on the part of the most recent wearer, on the quayside shelves of the Basse-Geôle of this great river port, thirty or forty *lieues* from the Channel coast, is that which immediately picks out the leather-hatted and wide-trousered seaman, *mousse*, or sea fisherman. No doubt, naval clothing, when it *did* change hands, changed quickly and locally, in the inns and taverns of the Channel ports. Indeed, the fishermen of le Pollet, on the far side of the harbour of Dieppe, and very much a community apart—most of them were of Breton origin—possessed a traditional *costume de gala* of such utter peculiarity, medieval in cut and colour, reminiscent of the habit of a court jester, in green, orange, mauve, and black velvet, handed down from father to son, and displayed only on the occasion of certain great annual processions, up to, and beyond, the Revolution, that its rarity would have strictly limited its negotiability to the restricted, inbred society of that secretive *faubourg*.[1] The livery of such proudly displayed particularism was unlikely ever to find its way inland, even as far as Rouen. Naval clothing, unlike *la défroque militaire*, does not appear thus to have travelled great distances away from the coast, even though it might have been seen in the China Sea, even in partial form; and it must be presumed that the many *mousses* who deserted from warships when they put in at le Havre or Cherbourg, took the initial precaution of shedding their distinctive clothing, before setting out for Caen, Rouen, Amiens, or Paris.

A study of suicide, violent death, and murder in Rouen or le Havre might possibly reveal some such naval components; but inland Paris, although such an important supplier to the younger elements of below-deck, appears very different, in this important respect, from late-eighteenth-century London, where immediately recognisable sailors are witnessed well to the fore of every type of collective disorder. Perhaps, too, such is the strength of the extended family patterns stretched over the whole of the riverside areas, at least as revealed in these documents, there would have been little inducement to former naval personnel (cabin boys apart), drawn entirely from the coastal areas, to have come to take their chance in the capital, unless it had been to hide. Normans of both sexes form an insignificant fraction (13 out of a total of 274) of the suicides—and most of these come from small inland towns and villages in the Manche, the Orne, the Calvados—while those from the west are even less numerous.

Yet what a wealth of information even the most casual of the *répondants*—the owner of a lodging-house, a *marchand de vin*, a *perruquier*—could read in an unhelpful bundle of very ordinary clothing, simply because it had been so closely observed on its wearer, in life! The rents and tears, the thinning at the seat and at the elbows at first sight would merely reflect a wholly familiar pattern of movement and of work, of standing up and sitting down, of bending over, and of

1 *A Sketch of the History of Dieppe dedicated to His R.H. the Duke of Orleans* ... *by an English Gentleman* (Dieppe, published by Madame Veuve Marais, 1832), p. 90: '. . . The dress of the better sort of the inhabitants resembles that of the English . . . but those of the fishermen & their wives present a striking contrast. . . . It consists of a red or blue jacket, short petticoat, trowsers, which reach to the knees & underneath blue breeches, with blue or red worsted caps on their heads & sometimes glazed leather hats. The women wear red or blue petticoats made of thick baize very short and full. Their aprons are either red or black . . .;' p. 118: '. . . the Pollet . . . contains about 4, or 5,000 inhabitants. . . . They were formerly distinguished from the Dieppois by the singularity of their dress. . . . These dresses are generally made of serge or cloth of one colour. . . .'

rubbing against a board or a work-table. Even the laundry-marks would have seemed better designed to mislead than to act as an aid to identification: Anne Marmet, 19, is drowned wearing a red-striped headscarf marked, in red letters, *L.D.*; Marguerite Merle, 21, is clothed in a man's shirt marked *P.H.* in blue;[1] a man with the initials A.M.L. has a shirt marked in blue *DD*; another, with the initials C.L.A., has a shirt marked *F.B.* and slippers marked *E.B.*; a 61-year-old *rentier*, P.F.G., has a shirt marked *B*, and so on and so on. Yet, despite so many obstacles, the clothes alone, or a combination of the clothes, the contents of pockets, and what remains of the wearer, will generally suffice to meet the needs, for once in harmony, both of authority, and *les proches*: a firm identification. It is the clothes that speak out, loud and clear.

One should certainly not be over-hasty to detect in such ready identification a heartening revelation of sociability, even of solidarity, of that rough, gruff fraternity of shared hardship, even of shared possessions (a complete suit of clothing, down to buckle shoes, hat, and gloves, in particular, being used, in turn, on alternating Sundays, by a trio of building workers from the Limousin, living in the same *garni*, and taking it in turns to stay behind in it, two at a time)[2] that may indeed have been one of the meagre consolations of the very needy. As we have seen, such familiarity was quite unavoidable. Even a family, immobilised in the dull, metallic legal language of the *procès-verbaux*, as if for ever dwelling—two generations—in the same room, would be huddled together more for convenience and sheer necessity, pooling their combined resources, than from the enjoyment of one another's company. Such constant proximity was as likely to produce a snarling

---

[1] '*Marguerite Merle*, fille de Pierre Merle, charpentier demeurant à Villejuif, âgée de 21 ans, disparue depuis 3 jours de la rue Caumartin dans une maison et chez des particuliers dont les comparants ignorent le nom et où elle demeuroit en qualité de fille de confiance . . . une chemise marqué d'un *P* et d'un *H* . . . cadavre reconnu par son père et par son oncle . . .' (procès-verbal en date du 3 frimaire an V). An unusual case, however, in another respect, as it is very rare for the *répondants* not to know the address of a girl's employers, nor even their name.

[2] See, in my *Police and the People*, where a trio of hatters from the Forez had the same routine. Some idea of the sheer *luxury* of isolation, of having a room of one's own, may be gathered from a promise made to a girl by her future employer: '. . . Elle est bien elevée & je veux répondre à la confiance de ses Parens, en la plaçant dans une maison où non-seulement elle sera bien traitée pour la nourriture, *où elle aura sa chambre particulière*, &ca, mais où ses mœurs seront en sûreté . . .' (Restif, *Les Contemporaines*). A more usual situation is described by the same author thus: '. . . j'eus une nuit l'idée de demander à l'un d'eux sa demeure, pour aller chez lui; je le fis le lendemain en rougissant; mais ce Garçon demeuroit avec 5 ou 6 de ces Camarades: il fallut abandonner cette idée . . .'

surliness, as a degree of mutual toleration; and the commonest form of crime to be committed in Paris during these years, as recorded in the papers of the Minister of Justice, is the theft of a watch, a watch and chain, a gaudy snuff-box in some cheap material, a checked headscarf, a handkerchief, a necktie, committed during the short hours of sleep, in a lodging-house, at the expense of the man or woman sleeping nearest to the alleged culprit. No doubt such objects changed hands over and over again, so that it would often have been quite impossible for a *juge de paix* ever to establish the original right of ownership. In such conditions, it would be physically impossible to conceal any article of value, clothing and small personal possessions being laid out, as if in training for a later, more public, and more carefully recorded, appearance, at best on a chair, a relative luxury in a *garni* (when Vidocq is invited to such places, he and his hosts sit on, and eat off, the bed),[1] more likely on the bed, the *paillasse*, or on the floor between two *paillasses*.[2]

Such conditions were more likely to produce a wary watchfulness, even at the expense of much-needed sleep, than any warmth of companionability; and such minor thefts are much more frequent on Saturday and Sunday nights, when masculine vigilance was dulled by drunkenness. Indeed, it would not be uncharitable to suggest that part at least of this apparently surprising willingness to take off valuable time—and *any* time, whether for work or for enjoyment, is immensely valuable—to come, sometimes no doubt day after day, to inquire of the latest arrivals below the Châtelet, may have been inspired by the desire to recover objects that had previously changed hands during the hours of night, the evidence of such thefts being thus conveniently revealed after death, as a posthumous Last Judgment on this earth rather than anywhere else. And the truly remarkable ability of a *marchand de vin* or a *limonadier* to put a name to a face and to a dis-

---

[1] '. . . On appelle un marchand de vin et, comme il n'y a pas de table, ils déjeunent sur le lit de Hotot . . .' (*Mémoires de Vidocq*).

[2] 'Quelque petite que soit une table . . . on y tient 3, sauf à mettre le pain sur ses genous; mais une couchette faite pour un, qu'on force néanmoins à servir pour 2, ne saurait contenir 3 corps; ce fut cependant le miracle qu'on fit faire à celle de Regret: on se met tous-3 sur le côté. Rose, qui était au fond, s'appuya plus sur un mur nu, que sur le lit; par ce moyen, on coucha, & l'on dormit collés les uns contre les autres. Regret, l'entendant souffler, étendit à terre tout ce qu'il y avait d'habits dans la chambre, fit adroitement glisser sa Femme dessus, la couvrit d'une serpillière & de quelques guenilles, & alla se mettre auprès de Rose . . . d'un coup de hanche, elle fit tomber Regret sur sa femme . . .' (*Les Jolies-Femmes*, V), sleeping conditions that would have been familiar enough to many of the *répondants* and the victims.

parate set of clothing, seen only a dozen times in his establishment, and once in the mortuary, does not suggest merely the professional conviviality of a man who lives off the brief enjoyments of people who are physically exhausted, and who turn to wine or *eau-de-vie* to see them through the brief hours of leisure. He needs also to keep a constant count on what he is serving, and who is paying.

Maybe this is to take too sad and sordid a view of what, in the last resort, is at least somewhat consoling, in a chronicle otherwise uniformly implacable. At least, for one reason or another, the *comparants cared*—just a little, anyhow, enough to have arranged between the three or four of them a time to go together (and some came from as far away as Bonne-Nouvelle or Faubourg Poissonnière) to the mortuary, in search of a workmate or a relative who had all at once disappeared, had not kept a pre-arranged rendezvous, or had simply failed to turn up at his lodgings. Why should we not be prepared to believe that working men and women really were worried about the disappearance of a neighbour, a companion, or an associate? There is a genuine warmth in the recurrent phrase: *c'était notre compagnon de travail, on travaillait dans le même atelier.*[1] It was not just the loss of a workmate or a partner, an economic loss if he or she were strong and willing; there would also be the loss of so much that went with work.

Companionship, at this deprived level of existence, would have to take the place of so many of the more sophisticated enjoyments available to the literate, the well-educated, and the affluent. *Conversation*—of the simplest, most boisterous, and bantering kind, 'j'sis v'nu à Paris gangner ma vie, & j'la gangne honnêtement, sans ête souteneu des Fiyes, comme Queuqu'uns d'mes Camarades' (this in the mouth of a *fort des Halles* coming from Saint-Germain-en-Laye)[2], often a well-rehearsed duo at the expense of others, or designed to attract the attention of a couple of laundresses, but not lacking in sharp, observant humour, and, indeed, memory—would have to make do both for a

---

[1] '. . . *Joseph Pages*, 27 ans, natif de Favrieux (S-et-O), ouvrier serrurier rue des Mauvais-Garçons, au 3me chez la veuve Deslandes . . . reconnu comme étant leur camarade de travail et travaillant ensemble dans le même atelier, rue du Vieux-Colombier chez le C. Bourdin, l'un d'eux, charon, par un autre charon, et par un ouvrier bourrelier . . .' (procès-verbal du 6 vendémiaire an VII).

See also: '*Gilles-René Lecœur*, tourneur en cuivre, natif de Paris, 39 ans, Clos Denis (Cité), . . . Jacques Claro, tourneur en cuivre, demeurant rue de Lappe, le reconnait comme travaillant chez lui . . .' (procès-verbal du 21 germinal an VIII).

[2] See Restif, *Les Contemporaines*. He goes on: '. . . j'vas lli chercher un fiaque . . . Pargnier! j'vou porterai comme eune plume, v'lez-vou? . . . j'sis orfelin d'puis 10 ans . . . j'avais b'n envie d'ête soldat; mais c'est qu'dans l'soldat, n'on n'est pas c'qu'on veut, c'm' – restant bourgeois . . .'

world of learning, and for the strident daily quarrels of the political gazettes. One could not in fact have been more remote from the Lone Wolf theme of the novels of late-nineteenth-century industrial America; and even thirty *hôtels garnis*, placed end to end and lined up in a row, assuming that such concentration could ever have existed in eighteenth-century Paris, which would have been most unlikely: rue de la Verrerie, rue des Lombards, rue de l'Hôtel-de-Ville, rue Simon-le-Franc, rue de la Lune, rue de l'Arbre-sec, rue de la Mortellerie, or rue Saint-Nicolas, would still never have added up to one Victorian Men's House.

The city itself, save in the new Divisions of the West, was as much a hotchpotch of considerable affluence and extreme poverty, often separated only by a couple of storeys, as was the clothing of those who crossed one another on the staircase (which was a point of observation much favoured by petty thieves, some of them dressed in sober black, with pointed black shoes further to emphasise their respectability, in order to account for their presence on the lower storeys, and who liked to operate in the early hours of the day, at a time when the servants of the well-to-do were either doing their shopping, or were gossiping downstairs, at the entrance, while their masters and mistresses were still in bed),[1] sweated together in August, shivered together in January, lived, procreated, and died, in close and uncomfortable proximity, in which nothing could be concealed, everything would be overheard; but in which, too, nothing and nobody was *indifferent*. That, too, is the language of clothing; that, too, can be gathered from these pathetic bundles, as well as from the statements of those who came to look them over, identify them, or claim them.

---

[1] *Mémoires de Vidocq*, p. 361: '*les cambrioleurs*: sont toujours vêtus très proprement . . . leur chaussure est toujours très légère; en été ils portent des souliers de daim ou des escarpins . . . en hiver, ils adoptent les chaussures de lisière. . . . Un *bonjourier* consulte chaque matin, avant de sortir de chez lui, *l'Almanach du Commerce* ou celui des *25 mille adresses*. Il prend les noms de 2 ou 3 personnes habitant la même maison . . . c'est ordinairement le matin, pendant que les maîtres sont encore au lit et que les bonnes s'amusent à causer avec la laitière du coin ou les commères du quartier, que les bonjouriers commencent leurs excursions. . . .'

(v)

Habituation to death

'... & the Jack-puddings, Merry andrews, Puppet shows, Rope-dancers & such like doings, which had bewitch'd the poor common People, shut up their Shops, finding indeed no Trade ... Death was before their Eyes, & every body began to think of their Graves, not of Mirth & Diversion....'

A Journal of what passed in the City of Marseilles while it was afflicted with the Plague in the Year 1720, London, 1754

'... it was not like appearing in the Head of an Army, or charging a Body of Horse in the Field; but it was charging Death itself on his Pale Horse; to stay was indeed to die....'

Ibid.

'All the needful works that carried Terror with them, that were both dismal & dangerous, were done in the Night; if any diseas'd Bodies were remov'd or dead Bodies buried, or infected Clothes burnt, it was done in the Night....'

Ibid.

'... The First of November, being the Feast of All Saints, the Bishop comes out of his Palace in Procession, accompanied by the Church des Accoules ... & chusing to appear like the Scape Goat, loaded with the Sins of all the People ... he walks with a Halter about his Neck, the Cross in his Arms, & bare-foot; thus he proceeds by the Ring towards the Gates of Aix, where he celebrates Mass publickly....'

Ibid.

'... s'est présenté le concierge de la prison de l'Ecole militaire qui déclare que dans la cour de ladite prison est étendu le cadavre d'un blessé dans l'affaire qui s'est passée cette nuit au camp de Grenelle et que l'on a apporté dudit camp de Grenelle encore vivant, mais qui est expiré en arrivant dans ladite cour ... un cadavre masculin sans bas, habit, ni culottes, ayant une chemise déchirée par force à ce qu'il nous a paru et un mauvais gilet verdatre, qui nous a paru être âgé d'environ 28 ans, taille de 5 pieds environ. Comme il est nuit close [6 heures] et que nous n'avons pu trouver personne qui voulut transporter ledit cadavre à la Basse-Geôle du Châtelet, nous l'avons laissé dans la cour, pour demain être transporté ... nous n'avons pu [en] faire [le signalement] à cause de l'état de putréfaction et du sang sorti de ses blessures dont il étoit couvert ... n'avons trouvé sur lui aucun papier ...'

'... le cadavre ... est celui d'un inconnu à lui âgé d'environ 36 ans ... cheveux et sourcils blonds foncés, le nez épaté marqué de rousseurs et de petite vérole, portant sur lui une chemise déchirée garnie de mousseline et bordée d'une petite dentelle, un gilet verd de velours uni, le dos d'une grosse toile ...' [d'après Chancy, commissaire des guerres à l'Ecole militaire]

Procès-verbal du juge de paix de la Division des Invalides, en date du 24 fructidor an IV [le procès-verbal reprend le 6 vendémiaire an V] '. . . Jean Quétin, cordonnier en vieux, demeurant Rue du Petit Carreau No 76, Section de Bonne-Nouvelle . . . reconnait le cadavre pour être celui du *C. Charles Julien Martin Morinot*, peintre et colleur de papier, époux en son vivant de . . . Citoyenne Marie-Madeleine Plumet, rue Neuve-l'Egalité No 312, signalement confirmé par le C. Saurey, cordonnier, rue de la Lune No 114. . . .'

So, for several days, the bloody body, clothed only in a torn shirt and an old waistcoat, had remained unidentified, a nameless and horrible object, rejected even by the two *concierges*, and caught, in a state of increasing putrefaction, which made each day identification more difficult, in an administrative and bureaucratic limbo, between the barracks of the Ecole Militaire, and the Basse-Geôle. In every respect, Morinot represented the odd man out, in a chronicle otherwise surprisingly uniform. For one thing, he was a 'political', a rebel, wounded to death in a collective act of conspiracy and armed defiance, and sabred by the military, by the soldiers of Foissac-Latour.[1] What had happened to the rest of his clothing, to leave him thus in this inadmissible state of semi-nudity, with his genitals exposed, a filthy corpse, wanted by no one, we can only guess; probably it had been torn off by the soldiers, as they might have stripped off the uniform and clothing of a foreign enemy, a *kaiserlijk*, killed in battle; and presumably they had taken everything worth keeping: jacket, trousers, or breeches, shoes, whatever was in the pockets, which, in the case of a 36-year-old house-painter cannot have amounted to very much.

A young man killed by the military belonged by right to the army; Paris was not in the battle zone; and such a spectacle was no sight for the Basse-Geôle, a place reserved for the respectable and strictly private dead. Furthermore, the man killed at Grenelle had, in his lifetime, lived in the Bonne-Nouvelle area, a long way from the river, well outside the parish of Bouille and Daude. But the *commissaire des guerres* attached to the Ecole Militaire could not—or would not—help; it was no business of his, either, the anonymous body, a bit of offensive rubbish, did not figure on his strength, from which there was no man missing. But, eventually, after about ten days which must have been days of rising anxiety to one or two people living in Hébert's old quarter, and with a wife increasingly alarmed at the prolonged absence of her husband (who, presumably, had not said anything about the rendezvous at the *Soleil-d'Or*, in the Grand' Rue of Vaugirard), and with the help too of a neighbour, an identity had at last caught up with what was left of the corpse, and Charles-Julien-Martin Morinot, 'peintre et colleur de papier', a blond man with a flattened freckled nose, rather under the average height, had acquired, if not a rightful place in the *procès-verbaux* of the Basse-Geôle, at least an incidental

---

[1] On the Camp de Grenelle affaire, see my *Terreur et Subsistances*, Paris, 1965, 'Note sur la répression contre le personnel sans-culotte de 1795 à 1801', p. 182.

place in the bloody history of unsuccessful revolt: a very small place, however, for this is the *only* evidence of the involvement of Morinot in the events of Grenelle; his name does not figure in the official report put out by Foissac-Latour; and he is not likely to be remembered in the company of such relatively celebrated people as Claude Javogues, or the former *maire* of Lyon, Bertrand, an omission which further emphasises the wretchedness of his horrible death. Even Robespierre, in the dreadful last morning hours of his existence, had not been treated merely as an object, as he lay on a Louis XVI table; he had been reviled as a person in his own right.

So Morinot had imposed his unwanted presence on a company where it must have seemed both distasteful and inappropriate. The Basse-Geôle traded in private tragedy, defeat, hopelessness, in private death. It was not designed to be a mirror to public history; even the two women blown to pieces by the Infernal Machine perished because they had been working late on Christmas Eve 1800 and had happened to be passing through the rue Nicaise going about their business. The accident of history had selected them as victims; they had not chosen the public stage. What happened to the bodies of the many other victims of the explosion we do not know.

Perhaps one could end up by *living* with suicide with much the same resigned habituation as one might learn to live with the recurrent spectacle of death. Yet such habituation does not seem to have induced indifference; far from it. We have referred to the wave of curiosity and horror provoked by the horrible murder of Saint-Saulieu; but even the murder of a poor female servant sleeping on the ground-floor of a shop was considered important enough to be mentioned in the press. Some of the awesome prestige attached to murder could be explained both by its rarity and by the fact that it so often took place during the most alarming hours of the night, between midnight and four in the morning,[1] the dread hours of *la Grande Terreur* of the Year II, when

---

[1] Restif makes the point that night would present particular fears to the sick and the dying man, who, during the day, would be prevented by the noise of traffic and by the street cries from counting the hours and the quarters: '. . . Tel à Paris un Malade aux abois, goûte une sorte de tranquillité durant le jour: le bruit des voitures, les *gare* des Cochers enrhumés, les juremens des Charretiers, les cris des Marchands-d'habits, des Crieuses de vieux chapeaux, de noissete-au-litron, de cérises-douces, de bouquets-à-mettre dans les pots, des pommes cuites; ceux des Porteurs-d'eau, des Vinaigriers, des Poissards: ceux des Colporteurs, des billets-de-loterie, des ferrailles-à-vendre, des mousselines à-50-sous-l'aune, des Vendeurs d'Almanachs de Liége à 64 feuilles; des Crieurs-de-mouchoirs, de peaux-de-lapin, de bouteilles-cassées, du papier qui dérouille le fer & l'acier, les pelles-à-feu, les armes-à-feu; ceux des Marchandes de plaisir, & de Celles de fromages-de-

even the most apolitical might awake to the stealthy step and the implacable knock of the *commissaire* of a Revolutionary Committee on
doors on the lower levels of a listening house. The experience of the
Revolution had made the night hours hideous as they had never been
before (indeed Mercier refers to the *soothing* effect of the four a.m.
clatter of the carriages of gamblers and revellers, as they headed for
home, a reminder of habit and continuity as reassuring to the *bourgeois
de Paris* as the hourly call of the Madrid *sereño*); and in the two or three
hours preceding a timid, reluctant, and livid dawn, when the decision
to kill oneself was so often reached, the memory of the Terror lin-
gered on in *chambres garnies*, as well as in well-appointed apartments on
the mezzanine or first floors. The crude violence of banditry and
chauffage was naturally confined in the main to the enveloping coun-
tryside; and the rural night was much more fearful than the urban
one.[1] But even in Paris, most—even the inmates of *garnis* sleeping on
straw mattresses—must have welcomed the dawn, however cold and
bleak (and Paris was and is a very cold place) as a promise of life.

Even so, Paris itself must have seemed a safe enough place, in which
the greatest danger to which the imprudent stranger might be exposed
would be to have his pocket picked or to find himself cheated at cards or
flushed out at the gaming-tables. It would certainly have been in-
advisable to lurk, after dusk, among the shrubberies off the Champs-
Elysées (where poor Rol had met his murderers) but the late eighteenth
century contained no well-advertised *quartier dangereux*; and if Guides
suggested that the Faubourg Saint-Marceau was best avoided, it was
because it was smelly and filthy, a place of tanneries, because it contained no architecture of merit, not because anything worse than the
contents of a chamber-pot or the gabbling of a drunk could befall the
well-dressed visitor there. The rue des Mauvais-Garçons referred back
to the medieval ruffians of Villon's time, the sinister-sounding rue de
la Grande-Tuerie and other similar blood-curdling street-names
commemorated ancient killings and bloody affrays dating back to the
cabochards and to the Wars of Religion; they were now streets in which

---

Marolles; tous ces cris, joints au tintamare de la claquette de la Petite-poste,
empêchent le moribond d'entendre le son des cloches & de compter les horloges:
mais dans le silence de la nuit, il n'en perd rien . . .' (*Les Jolies-Femmes*, VI).

   [1] '. . . A 300 pas du Château, au milieu de l'allée qui conduit à la grande route de
Caen, 2 hommes, armés de fusils, sortent du *Quinconce* à droite, marchent à eux
d'un pas rapide, les couchent en joue, et les tirent de 2 coups de feu, en criant:
tue, tue. . . . Bientôt on trouva le cadavre de l'infortuné Goubert: il portoit son
parapluie sous le bras gauche . . .' (A. N. BB 18 298, Justice, Eure, 6 messidor an
V).

even children could walk, if not in safety, at least in no danger of being murdered for their clothing. Even the recent experience of the Revolution, apart from making the night more frightful, had not habituated a largely apolitical working population (and the Revolution had nothing at all to offer the *habitant de garni*; it simply passed him by) to the daily evidence of political killing, most of the victims of the guillotine having been persons of conditions so superior as to have made scarcely any impression at the level of fifth- or seventh-storey awareness; and even the *septembriseurs*, far from being representative of the population as a whole, had been drawn from a small body of organised militants. There was nothing at all spontaneous about the dreadful three days of Massacres.

One might, on the other hand, indeed come to accept the fact of suicide; but even then very few would ever be involved in the family and neighbourhood awareness of self-inflicted death. Tulard's average of 150 suicides a year might impinge on 400–450 people at the most: not very much in a population of three-quarters of a million. And certainly the example set by the prestigious 'Martyrs de Prairial', as, one after another, they stabbed themselves *à la romaine*, on the steps of the Convention, or, by the 70-year-old Rühl, who shot himself in a locked room, was hardly likely to be contagious among a population of *commissionnaires* and *gagne-deniers*. Romme and his colleagues were expressing—for a last time—a sense of self-importance in a gesture of considerable political arrogance. They had always been arrogant. The news of their suicide could only have provoked a shrug of indifference among the population of the wine-shops and the *garnis*. Many might even have been pleased; for, by the Year III, most were fed up with politics and with politicians, asking only to be left alone. But, to judge from a memorialist of a few years later—1805 or so—the new Morgue had itself become a favourite excursion for a Sunday walk, a *promenade digestive* along the tree-lined quays, at least among middle-class families, for whom the wretched victims of drownings would have seemed as remote as the poor creatures chained to the wall in Charenton.[1]

The Revolution had no doubt deprived death of much of its accompanying plumes and finery; the guillotine was indecently expeditive and functional; and the tumbril removed the many victims of political assassination in a manner befitting a pauper, an inmate of Bicêtre. The 'Grand Froid' of 1794–5, and the epidemics of the three

---

[1] Jouy, *L'Hermite de la Chaussée-d'Antin* (Paris, 1814), quoted by Jean Tulard, op. cit.

late-summers of 1794, 1795, and 1796, had, like the political Terror of the Year II, necessitated rapid mass-burials in anonymous graves, in the interest of public health. The dead were not to be allowed to endanger the living. But, by the Year V, conditions had returned more or less to normal, at least in the capital; the claims of privacy and decency had been reasserted, at every level, so that death was once more to be accorded a modicum of respect.

(vi)

Conclusion

'. . . un habit de drap bleu uniforme revers bleu, collet rouge, boutons jaunes, gilet de peau de daim, culotte idem, bas de soye gris, souliers à cordon, une chemise de toile fine marquée *J.T.S.*, en fil rouge, ayant dans la poche gauche de son gilet une carte de sûreté toute déchirée . . .'

Procès-verbal en date du 13 germinal an VII

'. . . une cicatrice ancienne au bras gauche au-dessus de la jointure du poignet, un porreau sur sa main droite, la tête entortillée d'un madras rayes rouges marquée des lettres *L.D.* . . . une paire de souliers de cuir noir . . .'

Procès-verbal en date du 4me jour complémentaire de l'an IV

'. . . que son mari étoit absent depuis 3 jours et que depuis 15 elle avoit remarqué qu'il étoit inquiet et nous dit qu'allant ce jourd'hui à la Basse-Geôle elle a reconnu son mari aux habits . . . qu'ils avoient une double-clef de leur chambre . . .'

Procès-verbal en date du 24 germinal an VI

FURTHER than such occasional indications or comments the existing documentation will not take us. Those who draw up *procès-verbaux* that all have the appearance of having been written at great speed, and sometimes even in a crude form of shorthand (*s. à c.* for *souliers à cordon*, and similar short-cuts through the fastidious enumeration of each article of clothing and each item found in the wide pockets of aprons or in the less voluminous ones of breeches and trousers), and that are consequently often difficult to read, were neither concerned to establish motivations or to go into the details of the cause of an accident—it had happened, and that was all there was to it—nor to waste any time on the relatives or neighbours of the deceased, either with more probing questions, or with expressions of sympathy. For them, clothing was more important (because still endowed with a form of eloquence) than the clothed (or the naked), and once an identity had been established by at most four witnesses, there was nothing more for them to do, apart from adding such comments as: *s'est noyé volontairement*, or *s'est noyé par événement*, the difference between suicide and accidental drowning, in most cases apparent from such other details as: clothed or naked, time of day, month.

The *juge* of the Division du Muséum, an area of criminality almost as varied and as constant as the neighbouring Division de la Butte-des-Moulins, a steady supplier of *suicidés*, especially from the Palais-Royal and the narrow streets that approached that celebrated rectangle of pleasure, vice, gossip, rumour, panic, and staring, only set foot inland when it was a case of establishing the basic facts of a suicide, a murder, or an accidental death away from the river. What people left behind them in their rooms was beyond his jurisdiction, and one feels that when he *does* mention them, they are so pitifully few as to take up little time and space: *quelques hardes, un mauvais lit de sangle, une paire de mauvais souliers*; and if we are in search of notes left behind too by those about to kill themselves, either to explain their resolve, or to leave instructions for friends and relatives, we have to look elsewhere, in the papers of the *commissaires de police*,[1] and to a clientèle far more elevated and much better educated than most of the poor wretches who ended up in the Basse-Geôle: foreigners, anxious to explain their decision to friends in Brussels or in Antwerp,[2] and able to offer them-

---

[1] See Note O, p. 118.

[2] A.P.P. A/A 101 (commissaire de police de la Division de la Butte-des-Moulins, procès-verbal du 25 frimaire an V): '. . . les C. Barthélemy Laban, mar-

selves the relative luxury of a pistol behind the relative luxury of a locked door. The temptation to leave behind some such last missive must have weighed quite as strongly on those tired militants, men used to popular acclaim and unable to adjust to popular opprobrium, anxious to leave behind a political testament, even if it never went beyond the jaded eyes of a *commissaire de police* (or of a historian nearly two hundred years later).[1]

So one has to make do with such deductive evidence as is offered in *procès-verbaux* that are not intended to penetrate the inner springs of human motivation: age, occupation, sex, marital status, address, place of birth, length of time in Paris (occasionally mentioned, *en passant*, by a *répondant*, perhaps anxious to establish that the dead man or woman really had had *pignon sur rue*, was an integral part of the community of a quarter), all of which, when added together, or when examined separately, the better to bring out the oddity of a minute that seems out of step with all the others, as though the writer had all at once forgotten the formula, or had got bored with it, and had decided to set out for once on his own. It is reasonable to assume, for instance, that the minority of those described as *cadavre masculin inconnu*, or *cadavre féminin inconnu*, may have been strangers to the city, poor countrymen and countrywomen who had walked in during the famine years, in the hope of drawing on municipal charity. For it is hard to think of a resident Parisian being unable to muster up a *répondant* or two.

A torn-up identity card or passport represents a sort of pre-suicide, a bid to destroy one's official existence on paper, before destroying

---

chand crémier, demeurant rue de la loi no 1270, et Joseph Bertyn, rentier, demeurant dans la même maison ... que cejourdhuy entre 8 et 9 heures du matin la Citoyenne Michel, demeurant dans lad. maison ... avoit averti les déclarants que pendant qu'elle étoit sortie pour aller chercher du thé pour le C. *Corneille van Winghen*, logé au 3ᵐᵉ étage [il] s'étoit brûlé la cervelle et avoit été trouvé mort dans sa chambre ... un pistolet à côté de lui ... la citoyenne Anne Jeanne Henri femme Michel [déclare] qu'ayant fait auprès du susdit van Winghen les fonctions de garde-malade depuis environ 2 mois qu'il étoit dans cette maison, elle lui faisait aussi assez ordinairement ses commissions, que ce matin entre 8 et 9 heures led. van Winghen dit à elle ... de lui aller chercher son thé au *café du caveau* ... sur l'abattement d'un secrétaire que nous avons trouvé ouvert, une feuille de papier à lettre pliée en 4, portant cette adresse fraîchement écrite, *à Monsieur Borssekens, à la rue des Tanneurs, à Anvers jusqu'au 6 de l'an 1797 à Bruxelles,* le dedans de cette lettre qui nous a paru fraîchement écrite portoit *c'est moi, mon cher Borssekens, qui me suis brûlé la cervelle, ne sachant guérir de cette toux inguérissable, vous serez instruit sans adieu s'il se peut à l'éternité, votre beau-frère van Winghen, Paris ce 25 frimaire chez Laban No 1270 ...'*
[1] See my *Police and the People*, p. 357(2w).

oneself in fact. For it can hardly be taken as a clumsily pathetic attempt to mislead the course of posthumous investigation. Indeed, it presents the same ambivalence as the act of suicide by drowning itself: one *might* be fished out while still alive, there was a minimal chance of rescue, the card could be torn up, but the bits were never scattered, remaining in the inside pocket or wallet, an easy puzzle to piece together again.

It is questionable whether very much can be made of a detailed analysis of the occupations of male and female suicides, if only because it is so wide, and so completely representative. Luxury trades that have partially collapsed as a result of the Revolution probably tell their own tale; the years 1795 to 1800 would not have much consolation to offer an organist, a miniaturist,[1] a shell-painter, or a *peintre d'histoire* (history was moving too fast for such frozen attentions); and some of the employees of the monopoly institutions of the old régime: Fermes, Loteries, Cour des Aides, Compagnie des Indes, may possibly have had difficulty in readjusting to the changed pattern of employment and opportunity, especially if they were already in their forties in 1795, though a steadily expanding bureaucracy might have taken care of the more resourceful among them.

Perhaps here indeed is a clue to the enigma posed by this ultimate escape. So many of these unfortunates, native-born Parisians, with many years behind them in the same quarter, a good name and a good reputation, had become so fixed in their ways that they had been unable to respond to an expanding market of employment wide enough to include the whole of *la Grande Nation*, and to profit from the enormous opportunities opened to the quick-witted and the unscrupulous. It was not the Vidocqs of this period who would have been tempted thus to opt out, at a time when the going was so good, though they might get themselves killed in tavern brawls. Indeed, though among the murdered there might have been one or two with a criminal past, there is nothing to suggest that any of the suicides of either sex could be described as *marginaux*,[2] even the carters and those in transport are re-

---

[1] '. . . C. *Boischegrain* (*Louis*) 42 ans, natif de Metz, peintre en miniature, demeurant rue de la Tannerie, 46, Arcis, noyé volontairement . . .' (procès-verbal du 18 brumaire an IX).
See also: '. . . repêché dans le courant de la Marne, le 13, près le pont de Charenton, s'y étant noyé volontairement . . . *Joseph Bauny*, compagnon parcheminier, demeurant rue Antoine 299 (Arsenal), natif de la Ferté-Gaucher, 61 ans' (procès-verbal du 15 vendémiaire an IX).
[2] There is, for instance, only one suicide victim described as *marchand forain*: '*Louis Morin* . . . 32 ans, natif de Vimoutiers (Orne) . . . il avait sur lui une che-

vealed as having well-established bases. These were people who did not
have sufficient imagination to enable them to cope in a fast-changing
society, or who were physically incapacitated from coping. For even a
poor *gagne-denier*, as long as he had legs to carry him, could use them
to leave the trap set by the city, taking to the roads (as Swift might
have said of one of his dismissed servants: there was then nothing for
him but the road or the gallows), or joining one of the roving bands of
beggars active on the fringes of Paris. Many appear to have been as
much prisoners of their family and neighbourhood circles, of habit and
routine, as of skills inherited from fathers, mothers, and uncles.

Perhaps even the Seine, in its familiarity, may have seemed a des-
tination preferable to a step in the dark on the dangerous road to the
north-east. Suicide represents the total negation of the picaresque; and
it is surely at least of negative significance that horse-dealers and
horse-thieves should have been absent from our lists.

With women, winter suicides are rare; but spring ones proportional-
ly numerous, reaching their peak in Floréal, at a time of the year when
physical conditions would actually be improving. What then was there
about Sundays in May so fatally appealing to girls and young women,
to Henriette (18), Marie-Pierrette (18), Jeanne-Françoise (19),
Sébastienne-Victoire (19), Monique (19), Marie-Anne (20), Anne-
Françoise (19), Marguerite (21), Marie-Auguste (22), Marie-Thérèse
(22), Marie-Louise (20), Marie-Antoinette (28)—this last trio sad relics
of a time, in the 70s, or early 80s, when the Habsburg marriage, far from
being an object of popular loathing, was still being commemorated,
even at this humble level, or perhaps especially at this humble level, as
it is always one that mirrors the most faithfully the example of royalty,
in such imitative double baptismal names—Marie-Sébastienne (25),
Elisabeth (29), Marie-Denise (24), Catherine-Rosalie (31), Françoise
(33), as to induce them, though once baptised in hopeful expectation,
and sometimes in love, some indeed endowed with the manageable
wealth of three names, to retrace, almost step by step, as if in agonising
search of happiness briefly glimpsed and recently lost, the itinerary of
previous Sunday walks, and to throw themselves in *au Moulin Joli, au
Point du Jour*, and so on, or, curiously modern in this weekend
topography of semi-rural retreats, ferries, and shallow places, 'près du

---

mise non-marquée, une redingotte dépluchée brun, un gilet de molleton, couleur
grise de fer, un pantalon de velours de coton vert bouteille, une paire de bas de
coton blanc à cottes, une paire de brodequins et une paire de jarretières rouges . . .
cadavre reconnu par sa femme, sa sœur, son beau-frère . . . demeurant 1351 rue
Honoré . . .'(procès-verbal du 25 floréal an VIII).

moulin de Javel, vis-à-vis la manufacture du sel ammoniac'? Well, we
do know what it was for Marie-Anne, aged 20, who had drawn an unlucky card,[1] and for Marie-Pierrette, aged 18, of whom it is briefly
stated that she had killed herself 'pour cause d'amour'.[2]

Marie-Adélaïde, aged 10, fell in; so did Emilie-Louise-Charlotte,
aged 14. Adélaïde-Agnée, aged 42, was blown up. But Manon (70) (a
very old *Manon* then), Esther (64), Marie-Simone (59), Pierrette (52),
Bernardine (only 37), Armande (39), Marianne (56), Marie-Félix (45),
Marie-Nicole (51), Marguerite-Geneviève (34), and Marie-Geneviève (47) all killed themselves, in one manner or another.[3] Marie-
Alexandrine (31) fell down dead, in her room, along with several other
women, not all of them much older.

As we have had ample occasion to notice, physical loneliness on the
part of women cannot have had much to do with such gestures of despair. Moral loneliness, all the more acutely felt, for having been suddenly imposed, whether by masculine inconstancy, or masculine absence on occupations connected with the war, may offer a better ex-
planation. Not that marriage is revealed even as a temporary paper
barrier to such decisions; these were all years of exceedingly high rates
of divorce, as if to make up for a long backlog of shattered marriages,
and most of them operating to the advantage of male divorcees eager to
start again, who then remarried.

[1] '. . . suicidée en se jettant à la rivière pour cause de tirage de carte et de bon-
aventure . . . repêchée près le point du jour . . . Citoyenne *Marie-Anne Astel,* fille
mineure, environ 20 ans . . . demeurant chez le C. Sage, tapissier, rue de Sèvres à
la Croix-Rouge où elle étoit fille de confiance . . .' (procès-verbal en date du 17
floréal an IX).

[2] '. . . et s'est suicidée en se jettant à la rivière pour cause d'amour, repêchée
rivage de Passy . . . Citoyenne *Marie-Pierrette Dumont,* fille mineure, native de
Paris . . . 18 ans 9 mois, née le 11 juillet 1782, couturière, demeurant Bâtiment de la
Barrière de Belleville (Bondy) . . .' (procès-verbal en date du 18 floréal an IX).

Of another female suicide, in this case, a girl who poisoned herself, it is suggested that she was not in her right mind: '. . . *Françoise Agathe,* fille de Jean-
Pierre Feuchère, doreur, 29 ans, doreuse, demeurant chez son père, bâtiment du
charnier des Innocens, s'est empoisonnée avec de l'eau forte et du verd de gris par
suite d'une tête mal organisée et de prétendus désagrémens et lasse de la vie,
qu'il n'y a point de complices . . .' (procès-verbal en date du 21 prairial an VII).

[3] '. . . j'ai vu Paris, & je tremble, au seul nom de cette ville fameuse. Si une de
mes Filles—Claudine, Fanchon, Ursule, Jeannette, Catherine, alez préparer le
souper—si une de mes Filles y mettait le pied, je la regarderais comme perdue
. . .' (Restif, *Les Parisiennes,* I).

'. . . C'étoient les 3 Nièces, *Rodolfine, Albertine, Ernestine.* . . . C'étaient les
Aînées, *Dorothée* avait 20 ans, *Augustine,* 19, & *Frédéricque-Louise* 18 . . . *Constan-
tine* . . . 16, *Apollonnie* 15, & *Zéfirime* . . . 13 . . .' (Restif, *Les Contemporaines*).

Yet, with all these evident disadvantages—exposure to pregnancy, the economic burden of several children, a much more restricted mobility, a more direct exposure to the brutal realities of cold, hunger, destitution, the cruel jibes of neighbours, the cruelty of umbrageous brothers jealous of a family honour that they thought of themselves as defending, *par procuration*, through the person of their sisters, the Saturday night staircase tirades, followed by beatings delivered by drunken husbands or fathers—women still emerge as more doggedly attached even to the most wretched of existences than men. For every one *suicidée*, there are four *suicidés*, and similar proportions are confirmed by evidence from other towns. Of course, women would enjoy *some* advantages: their lives were not imperilled by the annual return of the military killing season in March–April; and, in Paris at least, they could live reasonably secure from the fear of the battlefield, and its attendant retinue of rape; they were safe from the attentions of enterprising postillions and persuasive cavalry officers, and they were preserved from the temptations of gambling and its consequences. Probably what ultimately deterred so many women from taking the fatal step was a more deeply felt religiosity than would have existed among men, more directly exposed to external events and to the pressure of the new orthodoxies. Indeed, one suspects that, with each year of Revolution, more and more women returned to religion, as to the one secure island in an ocean of uncertainty. Suicide was the most heinous of sins; and even under the Directory, when non-juror priests were still being exposed to an arsenal of Terror, there were still plenty of them about and ready to remind their female parishioners of their duties in this world and the next.

Suicide, even publicly committed, remains the most private and impenetrable of human acts. The historian is unable to interrogate those who went to their chosen death silently, leaving no literature, no testament, indeed, in most cases, leaving scarcely anything at all save a poor bundle of clothing, small change, and broken objects, useful or useless, keys that had offered little solace, opening either on to misery and wretchedness, or on to promiscuity no longer tolerable (keys that at least would see further service), the staccato *états-civils* contained in the records drawn up *chez Daude*, telling of freckles, warts, spots, dimples, a shapely neck, a cleft chin, shape of nose, colour of hair—features that must, at one time, have been admired, or at least noticed, commented upon, loved, even caressed—and nothing at all about the once-living person; and, somewhere or other, nearly always not very far away and not at all difficult to discover, a room, or a corner of a room, with nothing in it that would give the slightest hint of individuality. Most had travelled light throughout their brief, truncated lives, taking with them only despair and hopelessness, and leaving behind them a rippling pool of regrets and temporary sadness, soon wiped away by time and forgetfulness, as if they had never existed, or perhaps lingering on a little more in the form of a guilty sense of relief, as the result of the removal of the only other witness, apart from conscience, to something shameful and tawdry, to cowardice, meanness, lack of imagination, a grinding selfishness, all likewise soon smoothed away, to restore the even surface of self-esteem, habit, and the daily effort spent to obtain the satisfaction of the basic needs.

It was no great achievement in life thus to have killed oneself; yet the *suicidés* and the *suicidées*, though they leave us nothing save the inexorable fact of their gesture and the summary decencies of their tattered and darned clothing, are as much mute chroniclers of their times, in the dreadfully repetitive record of their failures, as those who kept diaries, who wrote letters, and who had sufficient self-importance to feel that their *faits et gestes* were worth handing down to posterity. Failure is much commoner than success, at any period, though it has seldom been accorded even a small corner in the work of historians; it is also more endearing, and much more human. *No* death can ever be dismissed as banal, even if it cannot aspire to the proud luxury of a tombstone—a bold claim on the future—and death at one's own hand, a pitiable appeal for attention, an appeal quite unheard, cries out in anguish for ever.

That, however, would be to end on too gloomy a note. The dead, whatever the manner of their death, stand in as pretexts to talk about the living. Perhaps, in our chronicle, the most important personages are the *répondants*, not only because they went on living, and thus represented the promise of continuity, but because their presence, their hints, their occasionally revealing statements and comments, open up a world of neighbourliness, of watchfulness, of enforced 'living together', which, however crude and brutal, noisy and filthy, quarrelsome and envious, was not devoid of compassion, tenderness, kindliness, and disinterestedness. Even the most deprived—especially the most deprived—set store by certain acceptable rules of conduct that enriched a brutal and often monotonous life with the reassurance of habit and the priceless gifts of companionship and conversation.

NOTES AND APPENDICES

Notes

(A) *Firing of pistols to the danger of the public, Champs-Elysées, D1 U1 48 (tribunal de police)*
Cases sent up for prosecution:

10 nivôse an VI (Sat. 30 December 1797)
11 nivôse an VI (Sun. 31 December 1797)
12 nivôse an VI (Mon. 1 January 1798)
12 nivôse an VI (Mon. 1 January 1798)
17 nivôse an VI (Sat. 6 January 1798)
30 nivôse an VI (Fri. 19 January 1798)
22 pluviôse an VI (Sat. 10 February 1798)
7 ventôse an VI (Sun. 25 February 1798)
14 ventôse an VI (Sun. 4 March 1798)
11 germinal an VI (Sat. 31 March 1798)
18 germinal an VI (Sat. 7 April 1798)
22 prairial an VI (Sun. 17 June 1798)
6 messidor an VI (Sun. 24 June 1798)
30 thermidor an VI (Fri. 17 August 1798)

speak for themselves: the firing of pistols was a week-end activity; usually young men, artisans, etc., practising against trees, endangering themselves and passers-by. A boy of 15 states (Sat. 31 March 1798) that he had bought a pistol for 30 *sols*, quai de la Mégisserie, and powder for 15 *sols*, borrowing the money from a work-mate. The culprit is an unemployed *décrotteur*.

A few weeks previously, 16 pluviôse (Sun. 4 February), the Bureau Central had put out a stern warning to *juges de paix* to be more rigorous in applying the prohibition of the use of fire-arms in a public place.

(B) Intermittent references from five *arrondissements* produce an additional 22 suicides for the period January 1796–October 1800. The records of the *juges de paix* of the other seven *arrondissements* have been consulted, but they do not mention suicide or sudden death. The dates of these 22 other suicides are: 17 nivôse an IV (Thursday) (D1 U1 35); 29 thermidor an IV (Tuesday) (D5 U1 25); 22 floréal an V (Thursday) (D4 U1 39); 1 vendémiaire an VI (Thursday) (D10 U1 7); 8 ventôse an VI (Monday) (D3 U1 7); 9 germinal an VI (Thursday) (D10 U1 7); 17 germinal an VI (Friday) (D4 U1 20); 17 floréal an VI (Sunday) (D4 U1 20); 25 floréal an VI (Monday) (D10 U1 7); 2 messidor an VI (Wednesday) (D10 U1 7); 3 thermidor an VI

(Saturday) (D10 U1 7); 5 vendémiaire an VII (Wednesday) (D1 U1 35); 12 frimaire an VII (Sunday) (D1 U1 35); 12 frimaire an VII (Sunday) (D3 U1 7); 19 ventôse an VII (Monday) (D4 U1 39); 22 ventôse an VII (Thursday) (D4 U1 39); 24 prairial an VII (Wednesday) (D1 U1 35); 20 fructidor an VII (Friday) (D1 U1 35); 3 frimaire an VIII (Sunday) (D1 U1 35); 13 germinal an VIII (Thursday) (D1 U1 35); 22 vendémiaire an IX (Tuesday) (D1 U1 35); 28 nivôse an IX (Sunday) (D1 U1 35). (Drawn from statements made to the *juges de paix* of the 1er, 3me, 4me, 5me, and 10me *arrondissements*.)

(C) '... repêché entre l'île de la fraternité et de la cité C. *Jérôme Maroix*, homme de confiance du C. Triple, chaudronnier demeurant chez ces derniers à Vitry-sur-Seine, natif de Morliac (Cantal), environ 42 ans, noyé volontairement ...' (procès-verbal du 19 brumaire an IX).

'... C. *Jean-Baptiste Donat-Duparque*, homme de confiance de la maison garnie dite du *Lyon d'Argent*, marié, rue Bourg-l'Abbé No 68 (Amis de la Patrie) ... natif de Foucaucourt près Amiens ... 25 ans 3 mois 12 jours étant né le 19 février 1776 (v.s.) ...' (procès-verbal du 11 prairial an IX).

'... cadavre ... retiré à Saint-Cloud, *Dlle. Vivant-Pensin (Jeanne)*, 27 ans, native de Genlis, attachée au service du C. Lapareillée, marchand boulanger et demeurant chez ce dernier, rue Montorgueil No 2 ...' (procès-verbal du 29 thermidor an IX).

'... Citoyenne *Marianne Brisette*, 56 ans, native de Navarre (Seine-Inférieure), femme de confiance du C. Duchêne, propriétaire, demeurant chez ce dernier, 432 rue d'Enfer-Michel (Théâtre-Français)' (procès-verbal du 12 pluviôse an IX).

'... noyé volontairement C. *Marin Richard*, homme de confiance, natif de Dorceau (Orne), 61 ans, demeurant Grande Rue d'Auteuil 24 ...' (1er frimaire an IX).

'... *Monique-Constance Monnier*, native de Paris, 19 ans 11 mois, fille de confiance chez Georges Ordunne, instituteur, rue Plumet (Ouest) ... une chemise marquée *C.M.*, un corset de siamoise à raye rouge, un casaquin de nankin jaune à carreaux blancs, un jupon de siamoise rayée bleu et brun, un autre jupon d'indienne à fleurs rouges, une paire de poches, un mauvais mouchoir de poche bleu et blanc, 2 mouchoirs de col fond blanc, dont un ayant une raye brune et l'autre à fleurs bleues, une paire de bas de coton blanc, une paire de souliers de nanquin, avec des rosettes vertes, ayant à l'oreille une petite boucle à mantille d'or et un collier de chien en argent ...' (procès-verbal du 12 floréal an VIII).

'*Marguerite Bilde*, fille majeure, native d'Autreville (Meurthe), 52 ans, ancienne fille de confiance, domiciliée chez son frère, Simon Bilde, ouvrier gazier, 1 rue Popincourt ... une chemise marquée d'un *M*, un bandage de descente ... [3 skirts].' Recognised by her brother and sister-in-law. It looks very much as if she had drowned herself because she felt she had become an encumbrance to her brother and her sister-in-law (1er germinal an VI).

'. . . que la citoyenne *Babé veuve Galland,* étant au service chez la citoyenne
Rossignol, chez qui elle demeuroit, rue de l'Oratoire, no 145, est morte d'une
chute qu'elle a faite de la fenêtre au 4me étage dans la rue . . .' (procès-verbal
du 24 messidor an V).

'. . . *Pierre Hardy,* domestique, disparu de chez lui sur le midi et qui a été
noyé près d'Auteuil . . . homme de confiance chez le C. Tapin, rue Villedot,
480 rue Thérèse . . . où il demeuroit avec sa femme, qui est cuisinière . . .'
(procès-verbal du 29 prairial an V).

(D) One might, of course, prepare for suicide by taking things off, by leaving
one's papers and valuables behind. The body of *François Jean-Baptiste
Daridon, dit Desfourneaux, marchand de vin,* porte Saint-Antoine, married,
two children, aged 4 and 13 months, is recovered from the river on 22
Vendémiaire Year IX. His brother-in-law, Berquin, also *marchand de vin,*
having identified the body, comments: 'que depuis 2 ans [Daridon] étoit
attaqué d'obstructions dite maladie noire, qu'encore que tous ses alentours
dussent lui rendre la vie très précieuse [we learn that his wife was only 26]
dans ses accès il ne parlait que des charmes qu'on trouvoit à quitter la vie, que
le 14 [a Monday] lui déclarant ayant été dîner chez lui, il en prévint sa femme
et l'engagea à voir un médecin, que le 15 [Tuesday, 7 October 1800] il passa
une partie de la journée avec lui Berquin, *qu'en le quittant il monta dans sa
chambre à coucher, défit sa redingotte, prit la veste dont il est présentément vêtu,
en tira sa carte de sûreté et tout ce qu'il avoit dans ses poches et sortit sur les
7 heures,* que depuis ce tems on ne l'a pas vu reparoître, que sa famille
inquiète chargea lui déclarant de faire des informations . . . qu'il fut à la
pompe notre-dame pour voir si en levant les filets on n'auroit rien trouvé . . .
que le maître marinier lui représenta un chapeau qu'il reconnut . . .' (A.D.
Seine D1 U1 35, juge de paix des Tuileries).

'. . . qu'un particulier venoit de se brûler la cervelle sur le chemin dit trottoir
de l'arche passagère, qu'il étoit de suite tombé à l'eau . . . *que ce particulier a
posé sur le pavé son chapeau, son mouchoir,* a de suite tiré de sa poche un
pistolet . . .' (28 Nivose Year IX, Sunday, 18 January 1801, 10 a.m., A.D.
Seine D1 U1 35, juge de paix des Tuileries).

'. . . que la citoyenne *Marie-Aléxis Manceau,* âgée d'environ 50 ans . . . a
disparu du domicile commun aujourd'hui [Sunday, 2 December 1798]
sur les 6 heures du matin, que dans le courant de la journée ils ont fait
différentes recherches chez ses connaissances, qu'elles ont été infructueuses,
qu'ils présument qu'elle s'est défaite, *ayant laissé, avant de sortir de la
maison, son argent sur la commode,* et qu'ils ignorent quels sont les motifs qui
ont pu la déterminer à quitter sa maison . . .' (A.D. Seine D3 U1 7, devant
le juge de paix du 3me arrondissement, 12 frimaire an VII, 6 heures du soir).

(E) It would not have taken very much for things to have gone the other way.
(Par devant le juge de paix de la Fontaine-de-Grenelle, 9 vendémiaire an VI
[Sat. 30 Sept. 1797], 9 heures du soir):

'. . . nous . . . étant au poste de la rue de l'Université, a été conduite par le
C. Charles-Pierre Duchorsel, artiste demeurant rue de Lille no 504 . . . une
citoyenne d'environ 22 ans, taille de 5 pieds, cheveux et sourcils bruns, yeux
gris, front découvert, menton à fossette, nez gros écrasé, lévres grosses,
bouche grande, haute en couleur, visage oval plein, qu'il a trouvée sur le pont
de l'égalité, marchant à pas lents, les yeux égarés, venant au-devant de lui et
regardant la rivière, qu'il lui demanda ce qu'elle avoit, qu'elle lui répondit
qu'elle avoit beaucoup de chagrin, qu'elle n'avoit besoin d'aucuns secours,
qu'elle avoit donné son argent aux pauvres et qu'elle vouloit se détruire,
qu'elle vouloit la mort et qu'elle la trouveroit là, en montrant la rivière,
qu'elle s'est mise à pleurer, qu'il ne l'a pas quittée et qu'il l'a conduite au
poste, qu'un citoyen présent l'a accompagné lequel a déclaré se nommer
François Dupont, demeurant rue des Pères no 63 . . . et à l'instant s'est
trouvé le C. Louis Jean Pierre Berthellon, demeurant rue de l'Université
no. 373 . . . vu l'état de convulsion dans lequel s'est trouvée la citoyenne conduite aud. poste, a offert de la recevoir chez lui et de lui donner les secours
les plus prompts dont elle avoit besoin. . . . Nous [le juge de paix] avons
accepté la proposition dud. C. Berthellon et avons fait conduire lad. citoyenne chez lui en notre presence et led. citoyen Berthellon a fait preparer un lit
et fait coucher lad. citoyenne laquelle a déclaré se nommer *Anne Gravier*,
demeurant rue du Petit Carreau, no 218, maison du C. Gilbert, laquelle,
vu son état de souffrance n'avons pu interroger . . . et le 11 vendémiaire
[Monday] . . . avons fait comparoître devant nous la Citoyenne Gravier pour
être interrogée. . . .

A répondu se nommer Anne Gravier, agée de près de 20 ans, native de
Paris, ouvrière en bas, et demeurant rue du Petit Carreau no 218, Division
de Brutus.

D. si elle avait eu le dessein de se jeter dans la rivière et pourquoi?

R. rép. que oui, parce que depuis longtems elle essuyoit beaucoup de
désagrémens de son père.

D. si elle s'est absentée de la maison paternelle?

R. qu'il y a environ 6 mois qu'elle est rentrée chez ses père et mère, qu'elle
est restée en service pendant 6 ans chez le C. Courroube du consentement de
ses père et mère.

D. Si pendant qu'elle étoit en service elle alloit chez ses père et mère?

R. que oui.

D. Si pendant ce tems elle a essuyé de mauvais traitements de ses parens?

R. rép. que oui, que sa mère la menaçoit de la mettre à la porte et que même
elle la frappoit.

D. Si depuis qu'elle est de retour chez ses père et mère, elle a vécu à leurs
dépens?

R. que c'est aux dépens de son travail, qu'elle leur payoit 4 francs 10 sous
par semaine pour sa nourriture, qu'elle se faisoit blanchir et s'entretenir de
son travail . . . et a signé avec nous . . .' (A.D. Seine D10 U1 7, 10me arrondissement, juge de paix de la Fontaine-de-Grenelle, an VI.)

The name of Anne Gravier does not appear later in the lists of suicides. Another recorded case of a suicide attempt being prevented also concerns a woman. (Par devant le juge de paix de la Fontaine-de-Grenelle, 15 messidor an VI [Tues. 3 July 1798]):

'. . . C. Louis-François Roland . . . rue St. Guillaume 1155 . . . [invite le juge] . . . de me transporter rue de Bonne [Beaune] no 592 pour constater l'état d'une citoyenne demeurante dans lad. maison, laquelle il a, ainsi que le C. Jean-Baptiste Roland [his son], demeurant même maison, et un autre citoyen dont ils ne savent ni le nom ni l'adresse, empêché de se jeter dans l'eau au pont ci-devant royal, qu'ils l'ont arrêtée à l'instant où elle se penchoit dessus le pont; qu'une multitude de citoyens et citoyennes s'étant trouvées sur led. pont, elle a dit qu'elle vouloit se noyer, qu'elle étoit la femme d'un émigré, et, l'instant après, a dit qu'elle se promenoit, qu'ils l'ont arrêtée à l'instant qu'elle alloit se jeter par-dessus le pont; qu'ils lui ont demandé sa demeure, qu'elle leur a répondu demeurer rue de Bonne [*sic*], qu'ils l'ont conduite dans sa maison, qu'étant entrée dans sa chambre, elle s'est approchée de la fenêtre, paraissant avoir l'esprit égaré, regardoit lad. fenêtre et paroissoit vouloir se jeter par icelle. . . . Jean-Baptiste Roland, ci-devant lieutenant à la 16 ½b^de de ligne, Roland fils cadet. . . .'

The next day she is questioned by the *juge de paix*:

'. . . a déclaré se nommer *Marie Anne Pauline Thulin*, femme de Jacques-Joseph Allard, émigré . . . divorcée en vendémiaire de l'an IV, agée de 29 ans, native de Pont-à-Mousson (Meuse), et demeurant rue de Beaune no 892, . . . et travaillant en linge et hardes.

D. si le jour d'hier elle n'a été rencontrée par 2 citoyens qui l'ont conduite chez elle?

R. que oui.

D. ce qu'elle faisoit alors sur led. pont?

R. que pénétrée de chagrin, elle avoit eu la faiblesse de vouloir se défaire, ce dont elle se répent beaucoup.

D. si elle a déjà eu ces tristes moments d'absence?

R. que non, que c'est la première fois.

D. si elle a des parens ou amis?

R. qu'elle n'a que quelques amis à Paris.

. . . Nous juge de paix susdit avons fait surveiller lad. femme Allard et attendu que son esprit a paru se calmer, nous l'avons laissée dans sa chambre et avons signé . . .' (A.D. Seine D10 U1 7). There were perhaps some advantages in being a woman and thus being noticed by the passing male!

Both cases are consoling as examples of an alert care and of a willingness to go to a lot of trouble on the part of people who were complete strangers and who happened (fortunately) to be where they were at the critical moment. They also illustrate the wisdom and compassion of individual *juges de paix*, particularly Nicolas of the Division de la Fontaine-de-Grenelle, a riverside area on the left bank.

There is an earlier example of suicide forestalled which also does credit to all those involved. A.D. Seine D1 U1 35 (par devant le juge de paix de la Section des Tuileries, 1ᵉʳ juin 1792): '. . . que cet après-midi sur les 3 h un quart a été remise au corps de garde . . . une femme qui venait d'être retirée de la rivière où elle s'étoit jettée de dessein prémédité . . . a dit se nommer *Marie-Jeanne Buisson*, native de la paroisse de Saint-Martin-de-Bazoches, district de Montfort-l'Amaury, âgée de 27 ans environ, domestique au service de la fille Fortier, tenant l'hôtel de l'union, rue Satory à Versailles où elle demeuroit jusqu'au décès de lad. Fortier et depuis logée à Versailles chez le sr. Machien, avenue de Saint-Cloud. . . . quand elle est venue à Paris? a répondu qu'elle y est venue ce matin dans un cabriolet qu'elle a pris à Versailles avenue de Saint-Cloud . . . pour quoi elle est venue à Paris aujourd'- hui? a répondu qu'elle y est venue pour se placer . . . à quel endroit elle est descendue du cabriolet? a répondu qu'elle est descendue au pont royal . . . pourquoi elle s'est jettée dans la rivière? a répondu que c'est par suite d'un chagrin dont la cause remonte au décès de la Dlle Fortier, sa maîtresse . . . qu'elle a été à son service pendant plus de 8 ans . . . que l'état de dénuement où elle se trouvoit, après s'être vue bien pourvue des fruits de son travail et de ses économies et la honte de se présenter pour chercher une place à Paris . . . joint au chagrin . . . l'ont portée au désespoir . . . si elle a quelqu'un à Paris, chez qui elle peut loger? a répondu qu'elle ne connoit personne à Paris, qu'elle peut se réclamer de beaucoup de personnes à Versailles qui rendroient bon témoignage de sa conduite . . . (considérant) que cet acte de démence pourroit en faire craindre de plus fâcheux si elle étoit remise à elle-même . . . ce que nous avons jugé par une grande altération qu'elle témoignait presque à chaque instant en demandant de l'eau à boire, nous disons qu'elle sera conduite à hôtel dieu pour y recevoir les soins de son état.' This was, how- ever, only a temporary solution, for, in her dossier, there is the following additional information: 'Thérèse-Mathieu-Larue, veuve de Honoré Alex- andre, coiffeur, elle faisant des ménages, demeurante rue des Vieux Augustins chez le S. Terray, maréchal, No 41 où elle a son ménage depuis 2 ans et demi a réclamé la fille Buisson, retenue à l'hôtel dieu, dont elle se charge jusqu'à ce qu'elle soit en mains . . .' A merciful solution.

(F) *Le Véritable Messager Boîteux de Berne pour 1796, '. . . Crimes atroces. Denelle*, de la Section de Popincourt, & membre de l'ancien comité révo- lutionnaire . . . fut arrêté quelques jours après [having killed his wife and three of his four children] à l'Hôtel-Dieu, où il étoit entré comme malade. Une femme dont il étoit connu, alloit vers midi dans cet hospice pour voir son mari malade. Elle voit un homme couché dans un lit voisin, qui prend des précautions pour n'être pas vu: la curiosité fit insister cette femme pour le reconnaître; il s'aperçoit bientôt que son secret est découvert, il supplie de ne pas le perdre; sa prière avoit été entendue par une infirmière qui questionne la femme: elle déclare quel est le scélérat. On l'arrête, on le conduit dans la salle des fous où il est mis aux fers en attendant que la justice en ait disposé autrement. Ce qu'il y a d'étonnant, c'est que ce malheureux n'a pas même changé de nom en se présentant à l'hospice.

'Il dit cette nuit à ceux qui l'entouraient, qu'après avoir commis ses crimes, il avait fait différentes tentatives pour se détruire; qu'il avoit mangé une omelette empoisonnée; qu'il avait pris de l'orpin & 15 grains d'émétique.

'Ce fut le 21 juillet 1795 qu'il subit sur la place de Grève la juste peine de mort due à ses crimes.'

Perhaps the point to be made here is the danger of going to hospital in the first place, not just medically, but at the risk of being recognised, either by ward-mates—and these might represent a pretty good cross-section of the population of the riverside Divisions, owing to the central position of the institution, but also because, being obliged to undress—perhaps for the first time in adult life, the secrets of identity would be the more readily revealed, a matter, of course, of indifference to the clientèle of Daude and Bouille. For the political significance of Denelle's murders and attempted suicide, see my *Police and the People*, Oxford, 1970, pp. 158–60, and 357.

Le Messager for the following year, 1797, perhaps predictably, has a long section on the *courrier de Lyon: 'Détails sur l'assassinat du courrier de Lyon'*, giving the following account of the flight of some of the assassins: '. . . On les a vus repasser par Villeneuve-Saint-Georges. On a même remarqué que celui qui montait le bidet du postillon [one of the victims] est resté près d'un quart-d'heure à la porte de la maison de poste à lutter contre le cheval, qui ne vouloit point passer outre, & ce n'est qu'avec beaucoup de peine qu'il a pu continuer sa route. Le cheval a été retrouvé la lendemain à la place du Carrouzel, où il est demeuré attaché la journée entière: les voisins voyant que personne ne le reclamoit, ont averti la police qui, d'après quelques soupçons, en a donné connoissance au maître de poste. Celui-ci a effectivement reconnu son cheval. On a trouvé sur le lieu de la scène une paire de ciseaux, où est gravé le nom d'un des employés de la poste aux lettres: cet individu a été arrête.'

The account is interesting as indicative of the vigilance of members of the public in observing anything out of the ordinary—the fact, for instance, that a horse was restive under an unfamiliar rider, that, later, it remained tied up for a whole day; so that horses could be precious clues to those who stole them—as well as the obvious clue offered by initials engraved on a pair of scissors. Objects were so important that they demanded such precautions; but such precautions could guide the police, as they can the historian.

(G) With the single exception of the elderly *cocher de place* who fell down dead in the street, on returning to his cab, after having had a meal *chez un cabaretier* (see p. 57), and could not be identified even through the number of his cab, all the unidentified corpses belong to the Years III and IV, the present *fonds* unfortunately not offering any such information for the Year II. Thus we have: 'cadavre masculin d'environ 45 ans . . . cheveux noirs en queue . . . un pantalon de drap moucheté à raies noires garnis de boutons de cuivre jaunes sur lesquels est écrit *République française*, et de dessous un caleçon de futaine avec des boutons pareils à ceux du pantalon, un bandage autour des reins, dans le gousset de son pantalon a été trouvée une clef de sûreté . . .' (19 germinal an IV); 'cadavre masculin . . . mauvaise veste . . .' (20 ventôse an IV); 'cadavre masculin . . . visage absolument défiguré . . .' (28 pluviôse an IV); 'cadavre féminin . . . environ 30 ans . . . le surplus du corps méconnaissable, vêtue d'un casaquin . . .' (6 germinal an IV); 'cadavre masculin . . . 25 à 30 ans . . . un bouton d'étain à cette culotte portant le numéro 61 ou 19, une chemise de toile ordinaire . . .' (12 germinal an IV); 'cadavre masculin, 50 ans environ, vêtu le tout très mauvais, sans bas et sans souliers . . .' (20 prairial an III); 'cadavre masculin environ 45 ans, bas-Meudon, mauvaise veste d'étamine beige, mauvais gilet pareil . . . chaussé d'une galoche à un pied' (12 prairial an III); 'cadavre masculin environ 60 ans . . . barbe blanche . . .' (6 prairial an III); 'cadavre féminin . . . n'étant couvert que d'un jupon de toile de coton bleu rayé très-mauvais' (10 floréal an III); 'cadavre féminin . . . une alliance au doigt, et une petite paire de boucles à lentilles d'or aux oreilles' (3 floréal an III); 'cadavre féminin 34 ans environ . . . une chemise de toile de ménage à manches plates . . . un jupon de flanelle blanche . . .' (14 floréal an IV); 'cadavre masculin d'environ 10 ans vêtu d'un petit gilet et d'une culotte à pantalon de toile écrue rapiécée avec siamoise rayée de différentes couleurs, un gilet de drap vert garni de boutons d'uniforme de différens corps, sans bas ni souliers, visage rond, cheveux et sourcils châtains . . .' (14 floréal an IV).

(H) On 19 Frimaire Year VII (Saturday, 9 December 1797) the *commissaire de police*, Lanier, of the Division de Bonconseil, appears before the *juge de paix*, to make the following statement: '. . . 'qu'un citoyen logé à l'auberge du *Compas*, chez le C Boujour, aubergiste, rue Montorgueil, lequel citoyen la nuit du 15 au 16 présent a reçu un coup de couteau dans le bas ventre rue des Deux Portes Sauveur à la suite duquel il est mort ce jourd'hui 19 sur les 7 h. du soir, qu'après avoir reçu le coup, le citoyen a été conduit au poste des Amis de la Patrie . . . voisin de lad. rue . . . [on] a fait conduire dans la même nuit led. particulier blessé en la maison du *Compas* où il a aperçu par ses dires qu'il étoit logé . . . [le lendemain] . . . ont trouvé led. particulier gisant dans son lit . . . malgré l'état de faiblesse où il étoit, ils ont su qu'il se nommoit *Jean-Baptiste-François Doesnel*, âgé de 32 ans, marchand, natif de Grandville [Granville] . . .' On the eve of his death, the *logeur* had had him moved from Room No. 11, on the third floor, to Room No. 1, on the ground floor, 'pour plus grande commodité'. In the room, apart from the body and clothing and luggage, there are a large number of business papers, money, and so on, in the stable, a horse belonging to the dead man; all of these are claimed by the victim's brother, Charles Doesnel, *marchand*, living in a village in the Orne, who came up to Paris, on hearing of his brother's untimely death, on 25 Frimaire. As far as the *juge de paix* is concerned, his responsibility ends with the raising of the seals placed on the murdered man's door. (A.D. Seine D5 U1 6, *5me arrondissement*.) One should admire, *en passant*, the considerate solicitude of the innkeeper in having the wounded man moved downstairs where he could be looked after with greater care and attention.

(I) 'un cadavre mutilé dont la tête est séparée du tronc, qu'ils présument être celui de *Pierre Saint-Saulieu*, ancien garçon limonadier . . . 35 ans, natif de Chaville (Eure) . . . domicilié rue Jean-Jacques Rousseau No 392, maison de Bullion (Contrat-Social), disparu depuis le 4 de ce mois . . . [le concierge] nous a dit que le corps du cadavre dont il s'agit a été déposé hier . . . n'ayant ni jambes, ni bras, ni tête . . . et que la tête a été aussi apportée le même jour . . . que le corps ainsi mutilé a été trouvé rue de la Mortellerie No 14 et la tête dans l'égout situé rue du Petit-Musc, ayant la corde autour du cou et enveloppée de deux linges sans marque . . . le cadavre est reconnu par le frère dud. Saint-Saulieu, François Saint-Saulieu, épicier, rue du Vieux-Colombier [qui fait remarquer] que . . . notamment le corps a un signe qu'il porte sur l'épaule droite, lequel signe nous avons trouvé conforme à leurs déclarations . . .' (procès-verbal en date du 9 nivôse an VI).

Whatever the tell-tale marks on his shoulder, both his brother and his neighbours vouch for the murdered man's respectability. On 8 Nivôse Year VI (Thursday, 28 December 1797) his brother—he has a second one absent in the army—and one of his former colleagues express their alarm to the *juge de paix* of the Division du Contrat-Social: 'nous ont dit que depuis le 5 nivôse . . . le C. Saint-Saulieu, âgé d'environ 35 ans, n'a pas paru dans ladite maison où il demeure au 4me, le premier escalier à droite, qu'ils sont on ne peut plus inquiets de son absence attendu qu'il est d'une conduite on ne peut plus régulière, cette inquiétude est d'autant plus fondée qu'il avoit promis aud. Frassard [ancien marchand de vin] d'aller passer la soirée dud. jour 5 nivôse avec lui . . .' A Christmas Day engagement with a former colleague was clearly not to be lightly dismissed. A locksmith is called to open the door of his room, only to find it empty, so the *juge* orders seals to be placed on its contents: '. . . une malle couverte en cuir à poil . . .' and, in the cellar, 'savoir 80 bouteilles pleines de bière, 190 bouteilles de gros verre vides, 2 bouteilles et 2 cruches de grès dans l'une desquelles . . . est un peu d'eau d'anis, une planche à bouteilles . . .' (A.D. Seine D3 U1 7, juge de paix du 3me arrondissement).

Vidocq remarks on the attachment to the observance of the traditional feast-days on the part of criminal elements: '. . . Le 31 décembre 1812, Vidocq, instruit qu'une blanchisseuse lui avait donné asile ainsi qu'à son frère, pensa que, par reconnaissance, Delvèze ne manquerait pas d'aller lui souhaiter la bonne année. Cette femme demeuroit rue des Grésillons, faubourg Saint-Honoré . . .' (*Mémoires de Vidocq*).

(J) D4 U1 31: *Renée Fouquez femme Lacour*, 44, 's'est jettée d'une fenêtre du 3me étage où elle demeuroit avec son mari, rue des Poulies No 160 et qu'elle est morte sur la place, que cette mort est la suite d'aliénation' (Friday, 23 April 1802).

D4 U1 31: '. . . un cadavre suspendu par le col à la rampe ou balustrade du palier de l'escalier du 4me et par un cordon de couleur bleue de l'espèce de ceux employés aux cordons de sonnettes, sur le palier une paire de pantoufles et un petit tabouret à l'aide duquel la personne suspendue paroit avoir enjambé la balustre ou rampe . . . est celui de *Marie Elisabeth Riel*, son épouse, âgée d'env. 63 ans native de Paris, laquelle depuis quelques tems était atteinte d'une mélancholie qui l'inquiétait, que depuis plusieurs fois déja elle avait manifesté des intentions de se suicider, qu'hier [Friday, 6 August 1802] sur les 11 heures du soir elle s'est couchée après avoir soupé en ville avec Augustine Marie Wirt, sa fille âgée de 19 ans, que peu de tems après lui Wirt s'est couché à côté de sad. épouse et s'étant endormi ne s'est point aperçu de ses mouvemens, que s'étant éveillé il y a un instant [4 in the morning] et ne sentant point son épouse à ses côtés, il s'est levé sur le champ, l'a cherchée, et ayant trouvé la porte de l'appartement ouverte, il est passé sur le palier où il a vu le spectacle dont nous sommes témoins . . . que l'événement parait être arrivé entre 1 et 2 heures du matin . . .' (procès-verbal du 19 thermidor an X).

D4 U1 31 (commre. de la Halle-au-Bled, 3 brumaire an XI): '. . . tenant maison garnie dite de la Paix, rue de Grenelle No 98 . . . qu'il y a un instant un *nègre* nommé *Daher*, au service du C. Pergaud, ex-employé de l'armée d'Orient, demeurant au 3me étage . . . est rentré et a pris une lumière chez le portier, comme de coutume, et monta à sa chambre . . . et qu'aussitôt que ce nègre fut monté . . . il entendit un coup de pistolet . . . et le trouva étendu sur son lit . . . le cadavre d'un particulier nègre âgé d'environ 19 ans, vêtu d'un pantalon rayé bleu blanc et rouge, d'un habit bleu national à boutons jaunes, et d'un gilet blanc, ayant des bottes à ses jambes . . . une playe couverte de sang et de forme ronde au bas de l'estomac, la chemise et le gilet brûlés à cet endroit . . . aux pieds de ce cadavre un pistolet ne portant aucune marque . . . lequel nous a paru neuf . . . Pergaud, propriétaire du nègre défunt lequel il nous a dit être le nommé *Daher*, sans autre nom, à son service depuis 4 ans, l'ayant acquis en Egypte . . . que ce particulier défunt lui avoit volé il y a 4 à 5 jours environ 12 écus de 3 francs, qu'alors [il] lui en fit des reproches et lui défendit de sortir, mais que malgré cette défense [il] est sorti aujourd'hui, qu'il ne peut attribuer la cause de ce suicide qu'à ce motif et *au caractère naturel de ces hommes qui ne tiennent pas à la vie*. . . .' Poor *Daher*, dressed up by his master, like a clown, in the national colours, and who must have cut quite a remarkable figure (Monday, 25 October 1802, 11.45 in the evening).

An apprentice, aged 15, to Busset, *marchand épicier*, rue des Fourreurs 459: 'qui nous a dit être entré le jour d'hier chez led. Busset en qualité de garçon et nous a dit qu'il y a environ 2 heures [8 a.m.] il a vu le C. Busset se raser dans son arrière-boutique, qu'un instant après il l'a vu passer dans sa cour, qu'ayant remarqué dès hier que led. C. Busset avait la raison altérée, il a regardé ce qu'il faisoit dans cette cour, mais a remarqué que la porte étoit fermée et n'a pas voulu y entrer dans la crainte de le déranger, attendu que dans cette cour sont des lieux d'aisance, qu'il étoit inquiet de ne pas le voir reparoître, qu'un instant après un C. habitant de cette maison s'est plaint [de ce que] la cour étoit remplie de sang . . . ils ont suivi les traces de sang et ont aperçu le C. Busset couché dans sa cave au pied de l'escalier . . . ledit Busset est veuf, qu'il a 2 enfants mineurs en pension à Clermont (Oise) . . .' D4 U1 31 (commissaire des Marchés, 9 brumaire an XI [Sunday, 31 October 1802]).

(K) The *répondant* was not necessarily to blame for an intolerable home life. A.D. Seine D3 U1 7 (par devant le juge de paix de la Division du Contrat-Social, 22 vendémiaire an VI): '. . . Je soussigné que dans la nuit du 17 au 18 . . . ma femme étoit couchée toute habillée dans son lit et que dans la nuit elle n'a fait que parler toute la nuit en disant que moi, mon frère, ma sœur Potin et Crussy nous voulions lui couper la langue, les bras, les jambes, les mains, et mille autres choses de cette nature, que je ne lui ai répondu aucun mot à tout cela, mais que vers les 7 à 8 heures du matin elle tombe sur moi qui étoit dans mon lit pour me prendre la clef de la porte, disant que je lui avais ôté la nuit toutes ses clefs, ouvre la croisée, se jette sur moi qui, tout nu et en chemise, attrappe ma culotte, que j'eus toutes les peines du monde à faire quitter, voulant absolument à toute force que je lui remette la clef de la porte que je ne lui ai pas ôtée et que je n'ai même pas, disant toujours que je voulois la mettre à la porte avec rien, et s'est mise dès ce moment à vouloir ôter la serrure, à quoi elle est venue à bout malgré qu'elle étoit posée avec de fortes vices et bien rivée, ce qui fait que je ne peux plus aller coucher chez moi car je crains que la nuit elle ne me porte quelque mauvais coup, je vous prie citoyen juge de paix de vouloir bien me donner les avis que vous croirez nécessaires dans la circonstance fâcheuse où je me trouve, car je suis réduit au plus grand désespoir. Matrat.'
 'je soussigné C. Boiron et son épouse, demeurant rue du Four chez l'épicier tout en face du C. Matrat, certifie que sa femme depuis quelque tems dit à tous ceux qui veulent l'entendre que son mari la laisse manquer de tout, tandis qu'au contraire nous la voyons de nos croisées qui ne fait que manger toute la journée et que son mari est obligé de lui aller chercher tout ce qu'il faut pour sa nourriture attendu qu'elle ne veut pas mettre les pieds dehors, disant qu'il y a des mouchards appostés tout autour du quartier pour la prendre et qu'elle n'est pas si bête de sortir. Boiron, femme Boiron.'
 'je soussigné que le 24 fructidor dr . . . le C. Matrat est venu chez moi pour faire ouvrir sa porte que sa femme avait refusé de lui ouvrir . . . elle ouvre les croisées avec précipitation en jurant des sacré nom de dieu non tu ne l'auras pas et le premier qui m'approchera je lui enfonce le couteau dans le ventre qu'elle tenoit dans les mains, criant à tue-tête que je voulois la mettre à la porte avec rien du tout pour donner tout ce que j'ai à mes parents et lui donner le fouet, que je l'avais dénoncée à la police et qu'il y avoit dans le café du coin 3 mouchards pour la prendre qui avoient de grandes redingottes, des capuchons par-dessus leurs têtes, et chacun une poignée de verges pour lui donner le fouet, mais qu'elle n'était pas si bête de sortir. approuvé Riffaut.'

'. . . qu'il y avait des mouchards appostés dans le quartier pour la prendre, mais qu'elle n'était pas si bête de sortir, de sorte que le C Matrat se trouve réduit à ne pouvoir travailler, étant obligé de lui aller chercher tout ce qu'elle a besoin pour sa nourriture . . . approuvé Riffaut.'

'je soussigné certifie que la citoyenne Matrat, à plusieurs reprises, a frappé à ma croisée pour m'inviter à chasser des mouchards qui se trouvaient au café au coin de la rue des Deux Ecus, me disant qu'ils étaient postés là pour l'arrêter par ordre de son mari, mais qu'elle ne sortiroit pas de chez elle, et qu'il y en avoit qui avoient des capuchons avec des poignées de verges, ce qui m'a paru un cerveau dérangé et a signé Lassagne.'

The wife of Matrat, a building carpenter, 461 rue du Four Saint-Honoré, Marie-Thérèse Chanès, 35, native of Ribencourt (Vosges), 'prévenue de s'être suicidée avec un rasoir trouvé à côté de son cadavre . . . le 21 vendémiaire an VI' (Thursday, 12 October 1797). She had been under medical treatment for 'une maladie latente', but had refused to go on seeing the doctor and to take the medicine prescribed for her. Matrat appears to have been a man of substance.

(L) A.D. Seine D6 U1 3 (juge de paix de la Section des Gravilliers, tutelle, thermidor an II—floréal an III). See, for instance, the *procès-verbal* for 2me sansculottide de l'an II: '. . . Caroline Anastasie Joséphine Blaise, âgée de 11 ans, fille de Louis-Henri-Marie Blaise et de Louise Riquet, son épouse, demeurant rue des Fontaines no. 10, laquelle a été condamnée et exécutée le 29 messidor, et le mari absent depuis le 1er janvier 1789, lequel a été considéré comme émigré. Savoir le C. Jacques Thibault, concierge du C. Lempereur, demeurant aux Clayes, près de Versailles . . . oncle paternel de lad. mineure . . . Jean-Baptiste Vacosin, tapissier, rue Phélippeaux, no. 24, ami; Antoine-Claude Bellier, officier de santé, rue du Temple no. 126, ami; Pierre René, limonadier, rue du Temple No. 128, ami; Pierre-Robert Huron, citoyen, rue des Fontaines, no. 35, ami; Pierre-Augustin Huron, ibid., ami. . . .' See also that for 18 floréal an III: '. . . la citoyenne Marie-Françoise Nicolas, femme divorcée d'avec Jean-Charles César Boucher, orfèvre . . . que trouvant l'occasion d'établir et de marier avantageusement le C. Pierre-Charles Boucher, son fils . . . mineur . . . âgé de 18 ans . . . attendu l'absence dud. Boucher son père . . . que le bon ordre et le maintien des bonnes mœurs engagent à favoriser une aussi bonne union, considérant enfin qu'il ne serait pas juste que l'absence dud. Boucher père depuis 2 ans environ pût retarder . . . un mariage . . . qui leur parait avantageux. . . .' The *conseils de tutelle* offer invaluable insight into the sociability of a restricted neighbourhood. Unfortunately, they only exist for a few scattered Sections of Paris in the Archives de la Seine (*fonds des justices de paix*).

(M) A.D. Seine D1 U1 35 (Tuileries, par devant le juge de paix, 23 pluviôse an IX). The principal *locataire* of No. 513 rue Nicaise 'nous a témoigné l'inquiétude qu'il avoit de l'absence du C Boucher, ouvrier au tabac, que depuis 2 jours on ne voit point paroître led. Boucher, que comme il est sujet à tomber en apopléxie, il craint qu'il ne soit mort . . . la portière . . . s'est informée à la ferme du tabac, et chez le C Provost, aubergiste, chez lequel led. Boucher avoit coutume de prendre ses repas, si on ne l'avoit point vu, elle a appris que led. Boucher n'étoit point paru depuis 2 jours, qu'elle présume que led. Boucher pourroit bien être mort dans sa chambre, vu son grand âge et ses infirmités . . .' The body of Thomas Leboucher is discovered on his bed, in a room on the third storey. A good example of a solicitude, practical, intelligent in that it drew on the old man's habits and frequentations, and unsentimental.

The individual habits of neighbours were so closely observed that even a short absence would not pass unnoticed and would be a cause for anxiety on the part of workmates and friends. Thus 16 Nivôse Year VII (Saturday, 5 January 1799), Mathieu Spong, *culottier*, reports to the *juge de paix* of the Tuileries that for the last five days Hiot, *dit Messin*—presumably then like Spong a man from the east—has not turned up to work. This is confirmed by a neighbour living on the third floor who normally hears Hiot, when he comes in after work, about 9 p.m., to his room on the floor above. So the *juge*, the neighbour, and a locksmith come up to the room on the fourth floor, 203 rue Froidmanteau, where they find Hiot, who states that he had been away for a few days on a visit to Bourg-l'Egalité (Bourg-la-Reine) (A.D. Seine D1 U1 35, juge de paix des Tuileries, 1ᵉʳ arrondissement).

'. . . a dit que depuis un quart d'heure un homme à lui inconnu, pris de vin, ayant tombé plusieurs fois rue des Lombards, a été ramassé, relevé par les commissionnaires du coin, assis sur une chaise dont il est tombé par terre, enfin ne donne plus aucun signe de vie . . . il est mort de la suite d'une ivresse très forte laquelle aura porté au cerveau le sang avec force. . . .' This happened, of course, on a Monday, 30 May 1803 (Procès-verbal du commissaire des Lombards en date du 10 prairial an XI) (D4 U1 31).

(N) A.N. BB 18 822, Justice, Seine-et-Marne, 'jugement rendu par le tribunal de police correctionnelle de Meaux, contre *Marie-Denise Toutain*, femme de Simon Moreau, charpentier, demeurant à Paris, Grande Rue du Faubourg Denis, 54, et *Antoinette Toutain*, fille majeure, sœur de la femme Moreau, inculpées d'avoir exposé à la vente à la foire de Meaux tenue le 27 floréal an IV [Monday, 16 May 1796] différents objets de vêtements &ca sans être munies de patentes . . . consistant en . . . 82 pièces tant en poches de femmes, jupes, jupons, casaquins, culottes & gilets, vestes, mouchoirs, un restant de pièce d'étoffes, peintes de jouy, enveloppé de toiles et langes d'enfant, le tout tant toiles peintes de laine, coutil et autres étoffes, le tout vieux à l'exception de la pièce de jouy à l'usage d'hommes, femmes et enfans, lesd. bas de coton fil et laine aussi vieux, toutes lesquelles pièces renfermées dans un ballot et liées avec une corde. A lad. femme Moreau, en 44 pièces de différentes étoffes tant à l'usage d'hommes, femmes & enfans, tant vieux que neufs et de couleur consistant en vestes, gilets, manteaux, casaques et jupons, toutes lesquelles

pièces ont pareillement été renfermées dans un morceau de tapisserie liée
d'une corde. . . . Françoise-Geneviève Maréchal veuve marchande fripière et
munie de patente . . . a déclaré que dans le paquet contenant les marchandises
de la femme Moreau . . . les pantalons et le manteau lui apartenoient, les ayant
elle-même donnés à la femme Moreau qui n'avait pas beaucoup de marchandises pour les vendre . . . la femme Moreau [déclare] que le commerce qu'elle
fait est si peu conséquent qu'elle n'avait pas à être assujettie à prendre une
patente. Le C. Perrot, défenseur officieux . . . a dit que la femme Moreau,
mère de famille qui ne possède rien et qui n'a exposé en vente que le peu
d'effets provenans de son mari et d'elle est des marchandises qui lui étoient
confiées à vendre par une marchande patentée . . . qu'elle est obligée de
vendre pour alimenter sa famille . . . que la fille Toutain, indigente et astro-
piée, est hors d'état de gagner sa vie autrement qu'en faisant par elle-même
des hardes d'enfans . . . qu'elle a l'habitude d'aller dans les marchés de Paris
et aux environs et que jamais on ne lui a demandé si elle en étoit munie, que
les femmes Moreau et fille Toutain sont comme beaucoup de citoyennes de
toutes les communes de la République qui comme elles fabriquent des hardes
d'enfans avec de vieux linges qu'elles se procurent, hors d'état de payer la
moindre patente, le fond de commerce de la plupart d'entr'elles n'équivalant
pas au prix de la plus petite patente . . . la citoyenne Maréchal . . . demeurant
à Paris, rue de la Lingerie . . . a dit que la femme Moreau est son ouvrière. . . .'

(O) D4 U1 31, commre. de la Halle-au-Bled, 8 prairial an X: '. . . Le suicide
du nommé Jean-François Gilbert, maison garnie des fermes, rue du Bouloy
. . . 1. que led. Gilbert est entré à l'hôtel des fermes le 1er du pt. mois, vers 11
heures du soir, et qu'après avoir demandé du sucre et du vin blanc, il s'est
enfermé dans la chambre qu'on lui avait destinée où il a bu un verre de vin
blanc dans lequel il a délayé de l'opium; 2. qu'il a écrit au C. Gilbert, md.
libraire, quay Malaquay, son cousin, une lettre par laquelle il annonçoit
l'intention de se détruire. 3. qu'il a écrit pareille lettre au C. Fion, homme de
loi, rue des Arcis, No 17 . . .' (Thursday, 27 May 1802).

D4 U1 31 (commre. du Pont-Neuf, 1er prairial an V): '. . . un petit morceau
de papier, paraissant écrit d'une main tremblante, portant les mots *déplore le
sort d'un infortuné signé Lequin, 22 floréal année malheureuse* . . .' (Friday, 11
May 1797).

D4 U1 31 (procès-verbal du 3 germinal an XI): '*Nicolas-Victor Bruyère,*
employé à la loterie, logé avec son frère, âge de 25 ans . . . ledit disparu de son
logement le 29 pluviôse dernier, ayant écrit au C. son frère led. jour qu'il
alloit terminer ses jours & depuis n'a pas reparu. . . .'

D4 U1 31 (5 germinal an XI), François Carzin, *portier*, 62, a widower with
one son: 'le défunt, disparu de son domicile il y a environ un mois et laissa
un mot d'écrit sur la commode lequel annonçoit qu'il alloit se détruire. . . .'

On 3 Frimaire Year VIII (Sunday, 24 November 1799), it is reported to the
juge de paix of the Tuileries 'qu'un particulier venoit de se brûler la cervelle
place de la Concorde, au pied de la statue de la Liberté'—a macabre gesture

of symbolism—'côté des Tuileries, C. *Carrey*, vivant de son bien, 11 rue du faubourg-Saint-Honoré [qui] s'est suicidé vers 9h 45 du soir: 1 stilet, une paire de pistolets. . . .' Pinned to his *dossier* is the following letter:
    'à Madame Feuchère, à Paris.
    'Paris le 3 frimaire an VIII, 9h. du soir. ne pouvant plus rendre heureuse une femme que j'adore, et qui fait mon bonheur depuis près de 5 ans, par l'effet d'un abandon aussi cruel qu'injuste des coupables auteurs de ses jours, je ne me sens plus de force pour rester attaché à la vie. J'emporte avec moi dans le tombeau le bien sincère regret d'avoir fait ses malheurs, et celui de mes amis, mais telle étoit ma meilleure étoile. Je la recommande, Madame et amie, à toute votre amitié, en vous donnant à toutes deux les derniers embrassements. Carrey.
    'J'ai essayé de réparer mes malheurs, le sort me poursuit sans cesse. On trouvera au bureau de prêt toutes les reconnaissances dans mon portefeuille, sa montre et 6 cuillières à café qui ne sont engagées que de ce soir pour 78 livres le tout, il n'y a point de reconnoissance de delivrée. On peut le réclamer avec cet écrit. Carrey, rue de fbg. Honoré No 11.
    'Je joins ici les billets Milhau qu'elle pourra réclamer. J'emporte avec moi la consolation qu'elle [—? —? the handwriting is very unsteady] quand elle le pourra, aux prêts d'amitié qui m'ont été faits.
    'Pour éviter toutes difficultés d'intérêt avec ma famille, je joins ici mes dernières volontés pour ma femme, ma chère femme puisse-t-elle se souvenir éternellement, sans nuire à de nouvelles chaînes, à l'amant et l'ami qu'elle n'a cessé d'avoir en son malheureux époux. On trouvera mon corps sur la place de la révolution près la statue de la liberté.'
    Madame Feuchère is Carrey's sister. He had given the letter to a neighbour, asking him to deliver it to his sister; but the neighbour had hastened to bring it round to the *juge de paix*. Carrey, a man apparently of substance, seems to have left nothing to chance (A.D. Seine, D1 U1 35, juge de paix des Tuileries, 1er arrondissement).

Appendix 1

Records of 4me arrondissement, March 1802–June 1803

In A.D. Seine D4 U1 31 (*juge de paix*, 4me *arrondissement*), there are a further 193 *procès-verbaux, mort subite*, covering in full the period 10 Ventôse Year X (1 March 1802) to 11 Messidor Year XI (30 June 1803), 16 months. Coming from an authority other than that of the Basse-Geôle, the minutes are both balder and less informative than the previous source, containing only rare references to clothing, and none to the *répondants*. The documentation does not represent the last stage of the journey, all the bodies quoted in the list being sent on to the Basse-Geôle, with which the ultimate responsibility for identification and disposal remained.

Of the *procès-verbaux*, 17 are irrelevant, falling outside the period, 127 are suicides (104 men, 23 women), 29 of them inland suicides, 98 of them in the river, 26 are sudden deaths, 23 are accidents.

The suicide figures may be broken down as follows:

Suicides by revolutionary month from 10 Ventôse Year X–11 Messidor Year XI

Ventôse X	(incomplete) 6
Germinal X	5
Floréal X	6
Prairial X	9
Messidor X	6
Thermidor X	10
Fructidor X	12
Vendémiaire XI	8
Brumaire XI	8
Frimaire XI	3
Nivôse XI	7
Pluviôse XI	4
Ventôse XI	12
Germinal XI	10
Floréal XI	8
Prairial XI	11
Messidor XI	(incomplete) 2
Total	127

Count by days

Day	Men	Women	Total
Sunday	13	3	16
Monday	11	3	14
Tuesday	16	1	17
Wednesday	14	2	16
Thursday	21	5	26
Friday	15	6	21
Saturday	14	3	17

Runs of suicides

Ventôse X (17, 19, 21, 27, 27)
Germinal X (21, 25, 27, 28)
Floréal X (3, 5, 7, 24, 27, 30)
Prairial X (1er, 4, 7, 8, 10, 13, 13, 14)
Thermidor X (4, 8, 9, 10, 18, 19, 22, 25)
Fructidor X (3, 4, 13, 15, 15, 15, 16, 22, 26, 27)

Vendémiaire XI (2, 6, 17, 19, 22, 27, 29)
Brumaire XI (3, 4, 6, 9, 15, 17, 26, 29)
Frimaire XI (2)
Nivôse XI (2, 6, 11, 16, 17, 18, 30)
Pluviôse XI (1er)
Ventôse XI (5, 5, 14, 15, 17, 21, 22, 29)
Germinal XI (2, 6, 10, 19, 20, 26, 26, 28)
Floréal XI (12, 15, 16, 17, 30, 30, 30)
Prairial XI (2, 8, 11, 12, 13, 13, 15, 18, 19, 27, 29)

Suicide by age group

Age	Men		Women		Total
under 20	7	under 40	3	under 40	10
20–29	16	= 54	6	= 11	22
30–39	31		2		33
40–49	23	over 40	6	over 40	29
50+	23	= 46	6	= 12	29
unknown	4		0		4
Total all ages	104		23		127

Suicide by provincial origin

Paris 33		(23 men, 10 women)
Paris Region	25	
North-East	12	
Normandy	15	
West	7	
East	6	
Centre	13	
Foreign	8	(Piedmont, Liége, Cairo, Berne, Wags (Brabant), Bamberg, Bouillon, Gothenburg)
Total	119	

As in the main dossier, Parisians or people from the Paris area predominate. On the other hand, there are more Normans. Over 60% of the addresses given are those of *chambres garnies* in the riverside Divisions, and repeat the addresses of the list in Appendix 3.

Occupations of the suicides

The shift towards the middle and higher age groups illustrated in the breakdown by ages in the later list is further suggested by the rather more affluent character of many of the trades and occupations as compared with those of the main dossier. There are a number of high-ranking officials, including one courtier, 3 *propriétaires*, and 4 *rentiers*, and considerably more merchants than in the earlier list, while the clothing, food, and drink trades are underrepresented. Only the women tend to represent the lowest occupational ranks: *blanchisseuses, couturières, filles de confiance, cuisinières*. Not surprisingly, there are more soldiers than ever. The general impression borne out by some of the suicide notes or the comments of relatives and neighbours, is that suicide had often been dictated by personal and private distress, rather than by economic hardship. In a number of cases, madness, depression, and pain are mentioned as motivating causes; and some of the notes indicate either the breakdown of a marriage or the loss of a companion as the deciding factor.

Appendix 2

Occupational analysis of the suicides and victims of sudden death

agent de change
armateur (négotiant)

baigneur (garçon)
balayeur
bijoutier
blanchisseur (ex-)
blanchisseuses (6)
bonnetier (ouvrier)
boucher (apprenti)
bouchers (marchands) (2)
boulangers (garçons) (2)
boutonnier
boutonnière (ouvrière)
brasseur
brasseurs (garçons) (3)
brodeuse

carreleur (compagnon)
chandelier (garçon)
chapelier (garçon)
chapelier (marchand)
charbonnier-porteur
charcutier
charpentier
charpentiers (compagnons) (2)
charron (compagnon)
chartiers (3)
cochers de place (4)
coiffeur
coiffeuse (ancienne)
commissionnaires (3)
commissionnaire de vins à la Halle aux
   vins
Consul de France à Philadelphie (ex-)
Cordelier (ex-frère, puis pâtissier)
cordier
cordonniers (3)
cordonniers(garçons) (3)

corroyeur
coutelier (compagnon)
couturières en robes (5)
couvreur
cuisiniers (2)
cuisinière
cultivateurs (4)

domestique (masc.)
domestique (fém.)
doreuse

ébéniste (apprenti)
écolier
écrivain
empileur sur les ports
employés (3)
employés (ex-) (3)
employé des postes (ex-)
épiciers (garçons) (2)
étudiants (3)

fabricant de draps
facteur d'instruments de musique
faÿancier
femme de ménage
ferblantier (apprenti)
ferrailleur
filles de confiance (4)
flotteur
fourbisseur (ancien)
fruitiers (2)
fruitier-crêmier
fusilier

gagne-centimes (2)
gagne-deniers (6)
gardien de musée
gazier (ouvrier)

grainier
greffier (ancien greffier à la Cour des
    Aides)
grenadier

hommes de confiance (6)
homme de confiance (ancien)
hommes de loi (2)
homme de rivière
hospices, habitants d' (3)
huissier (ancien)
huissier (clerc d')

imprimeurs (2)
imprimeur (apprenti)
imprimeur et militaire
inspecteur du balayage
inspecteur des équipages d'artillerie
instituteurs (3)
Invalides (5)

jardinier
jouaillier (ancien)
journaliers (7)

libraire
limonadiers (garçons) (4)
limonadier (ancien garçon)
loterie (sous-chef de la correspondance)
loterie (ancien employé à la loterie
    royale)

maçon
maçon (compagnon)
maîtres de danse (2)
manouvrière
maraîcher
marchands (commis) (2)
marchand de balais
marchand forain
marchand de journaux
marchand de porcs frais
marchands de vin (2)
marchande à la Halle
marchande de légumes
mariniers (2)
matelassière
menuisier
menuisier (ancien)

menuisier (apprenti)
menuisier (compagnon)
militaires (7)

nourrisseur de bestiaux

officier de bouche (ex-)
officier de santé
orfèvre (apprenti)
ouvrières (5)
ouvrière en modes
ouvrière en papeterie
ouvrière en tabatières

parcheminier (compagnon)
pâtissier (ex-Cordelier)
paveur
peaussier (marchand)
peintres (3)
peintre et colleur
peintre (artiste, élève de David)
peintre en miniature
perruquiers (6)
polisseuse (bijoutière)
porte-sac

ramoneur
regrattier
remplaçant
rentiers (7)
rentière
revendeuses (2)

sans état (3)
sellier (apprenti)
serruriers (apprentis) (2)
serrurier (ouvrier)

tabletière en carton
tailleurs (2)
tapissier
tapissier (apprenti)
teinturier (apprenti)
tourneur en cuivre
traiteur (garçon)

vétérans (5)
vigneron
vitrier
voiturier par terre

Appendix 3

Addresses established as those of *Maisons Garnies*

rue Antoine, au coin de la rue des Ballets

Hôtel des Indes, rue Traversière-Saint-Honoré

Le Lion d'Argent, 68 rue Bourg-l'Abbé

28 rue du Vertbois

32 rue Saint-Germain-l'Auxerrois, chez Gourdelle, logeur

154 rue d'Angervilliers

rue Marché-d'Aguesseau, chez Parquier, logeur

4 rue Gervais-Lanseuil, Cité

16 rue Saint-Honoré

Café de la Paix, rue de Viarmes

55 rue des Barres

rue Saint-Dominique, chez un aubergiste

8 rue Froidmanteau

rue des Poulies, chez Augéol, logeur

rue Coquillière, maison Touchard

rue Pirouette, maison Duheaume

rue des Cordiers

76 rue du Chantre

maison Bullion, 392 rue Jean-Jacques Rousseau

division des Marchés; no address given

618 rue du Contrat-Social, chez un limonadier

Maison Garnie du Parc, 188 rue de l'Arbre-sec

40 rue Saint-Germain

849 rue Gaillon

40 rue Quincampoix

Appendix 4

Suicides other than by drowning in the Seine

Tuesday, 16 June 1795. Louis Pillon, living with his mother, 75, rue des Fosses-Saint-Germain-l'Auxerrois, 'lequel s'est détruit d'un coup de pistolet'.

Tuesday, 21 February 1797. Jean Berleux, ferrailleur, '. . . duquel il appert que ledit défunt s'est tué d'un coup de fusil . . .'.

Friday, 16 June 1797. Briquet, 54, married but living apart from his wife, 'suspendu à une corde, mort depuis 4 ou 5 heures . . .'.

Monday, 7 August 1797. Louis-Antoine Thévenet, born in Paris, aged 34, 'ancien militaire, avoir été trouvé pendu à son domicile, rue Bertin-Poirée No 218'.

Thursday, 29 March 1798. '. . . *André Sauvé* est décédé le jour d'hier (29) vers les 6 heures du matin dans une chambre au 6me, qu'il s'est brûlé la cervelle . . . qu'il s'étoit enfermé au verrou, que le propriétaire et tous sont montés et l'ont vu mort, un fils de 24 ans étoit présent . . .' (greffier du juge de paix de la Division des Halles).

Saturday, 22 December 1798. Louis-Mathias Pérard, native of Moray (Haute-Marne), 's'est suicidé . . . rue de la Ferronnerie No 154'.

Monday, 2 June 1799. Jacques Gillet, ex-lieutenant, 1er bataillon des Ardennes, aged 27, native of Rocroy, living for the previous three months in Paris, 603 rue Helvétius: 'ledit cadavre a été trouvé avec une corde au cou qui lui descendait jusqu'à la ceinture.'

Saturday, 8 June 1799. Françoise Agathe Feuchère, doreuse, living with her father, a *doreur*, Charnier des Innocents, aged 29, 's'est empoisonnée avec de l'eau-forte et de verd de gris par suite d'une tête mal organisée et de prétendus désagrémens et lasse de la vie, qu'il n'y a point de complices . . .'.

Sunday, 10 August 1799. Jean-Baptiste d'Allemagne, marchand de porcs frais à la Halle, 45 to 48, 's'est suicidé avec un pistolet' (Marchés).

Friday, 1 November 1799. Guillaume Bourgeat, 4me étage, 233 rue de l'Arbre-Sec (Gardes-françaises), 's'est suicidé volontairement en se précipitant dans la rue par une des fenêtres de l'appartement qu'il occupoit au 4me'.

Saturday, 22 February 1800. Augustin Rémy Auvert, 'peintre, élève de David, natif de Paris . . . 19 ans et ½, fils mineur de Nicolas Auvert, rentier, 134 rue du faubourg Martin, disparu depuis le 3 [ventôse] 3 heures de relevé, il a été trouvé en bas d'une des tours du temple de la Raison (Cité) du haut de laquelle il s'étoit précipité sur les 4 heures de relevé . . .' The body is identified by his father.

Tuesday, 16 March 1800. Jean-Jacques Pinel, 29 rue Saint-Denis, aged 39, 's'y étoit brûlé la cervelle . . .'.

Saturday, 29 March 1800. Femme Mazurier, the wife of a 'courier du Département de la Guerre, actuellement absent, a été trouvée suicidée . . . dans le logement qu'elle occupoit Cloître Germain-L'Auxerrois No 39 . . .'.

Monday, 7 April 1800. Pierre l'Hoste, 'commis marchand . . . 119 rue du Champ-Fleury, s'est suicidé chez lui.'

Wednesday, 28 May 1800. '. . . s'étant suicidé le 8 du courant [prairial] . . . 4 heures du matin dans les bateaux à lessive, arche-Marion . . . *François-Urbain Léger* . . . 53 ans, ci-devant cuisinier, et depuis ex-militaire vétéran . . . caserné rue des Victoires Nationales . . .'.

Saturday, 31 May 1800. Marin-Prosper Arzon, 'marchand peaussier, natif de Paris, âgé de 47 ans, demeurant rue de la Jussienne, disparu de chez lui à 10 heures du matin . . . le cadavre a été trouvé suicidé dans le bois de Boulogne . . .'.

Friday, 11 July 1800. Pierre Robichon de la Guérinière, ex-gendarme, aged 50, native of Caen, living at the corner of the rue Saint-Germain-l'Auxerrois, 'trouvé baigné dans son sang' in his room.

Sunday, 11 January 1801. '*Louis Barville,* 18½, apprenti orfèvre, s'est brûlé la cervelle . . .'.

Wednesday, 25 March 1801: '. . . cadavre masculin lequel s'est précipité d'un 5me étage, rue des Petits-Champs au coin de celle Chabanais . . . entre midi et une heure . . . *Pierre Baubant,* fruitier, 37 ans, natif de Conflandé (Haute-Saône) domicilié 863 rue Traversière. . . .' He must have thrown himself out of a staircase window after climbing up to the fifth storey of a house in which he did not live.

Thursday, 23 April 1801. '. . . s'est suicidé ledit jour heure de midi dans les Champs-Elysées en se brûlant la cervelle . . . absent de son domicile . . . vers 9 heures et ½ du matin . . . C. *Pierre Desplans,* employé gardien du muséum central des arts, y demeurant, natif de Saint-Nicolas-de-Vérost (Mont-Blanc) . . . 47 ans . . . marié.'

Tuesday, 5 May 1801. '. . . en se brûlant la cervelle . . . *Jacques Dubois,* homme de loi, natif de Saint-Germain-en-Laye . . . 27 ans, marié à Mons le 15 nivôse an V, demeurant *hôtel des Indes,* garni, rue Traversière-Honoré, cadavre reconnu par sa femme . . .'.

Wednesday, 20 May 1801. '. . . trouvé noyé dans la Seine, ou se brûlant la cervelle, *Louis Aubrié,* garçon chapelier, environ 20 ans, natif de Reims . . . demeurant à Paris chez le C. Anne, chirurgien accoucheur, quai de Monnoie, au coin de la rue de Nevers . . .'.

Saturday, 4 July 1801. '... *Armande Boisvin,* manouvrière, dite *Desfresne* ... environ 39 ans, native de Paris, femme d'Adrien Boisvin, employé à la trésorerie nationale ... il résulte que le C. Boisvin étant rentré chez lui avec une autre citoyenne ... a aperçu le cadavre de son épouse attaché par le col à une corde, que depuis longtems cette femme avoit l'esprit aliéné et avait déjà fait des actes de démence ...'.

Thursday, 5 September 1801. '... cadavre masculin ... absent depuis le 9 fructidor, relevé boulevard des Capucines, lequel s'est suicidé d'un coup de feu le jour d'hier ... C. *Vidalet (Jean-François),* âgé d'environ 45 ans, natif de Mirepoix, département de l'Ariège, homme de loi, célibataire, demeurant boulevard Montmartre No 27 ...'.

Index of Place Names

NOTE: *Bicêtre* has been listed under Paris, as a Parisian institution, although situated just outside the city.

Alfort, 66(1)
Amiens, 80, 82
Antilly (Oise), 31
Antwerp, 50, 96
Arcueil, 11, 80
Aubervilliers, 14(2)
Aubigny-sur-Nère (Cher), 10(1)
Auteuil, 106
Autreville-sur-Moselle (Meurthe), 106 (C)

Bab-el-Oued, 36(1)
Beauficel (Manche), 14(1)
Beaugency (Loiret), 74(1)
Belleville, 67(1)
Berne, 27, 123
Bonnet-le-Louvet (Seine-Inférieure), 55(1)
Bouillon, 123
Boulogne-sur-Mer, 54(3)
Bourg-la-Reine (Bourg-l'Egalité), 117
Brosse (la) (Seine-et-Oise), 49(1)
Bruges, 80
Brussels, 61(2), 80, 96
Budling (Moselle), 49(2)

Caen, 82, 91(1), 128
Cairo, 123
Cappy (Oise), 19(1)
Chaillot, 48, 51, 71(1)
Champaigne (Cantal), 75(1)
Chapelle (la), 12, 80
Charenton, 49(3), 92

Charleville, 60
Châteauroux, 14
Châtillon-sur-Indre, 37(1)
Châtillon-sur-Orge, 49(3)
Cherbourg, 82
Clamart, 20(2)
Clermont-Ferrand, 21(2)
Clignancourt, 11, 12, 75(1), 80
Cologne, 51, 80
Compiègne, 31(1)

Délemont, 62
Dieppe, 73, 81, 82(1)
Dorceau (Orne), 106
Dordrecht, 80
Douai, 27(2)
Dunkirk, 76(1)

Evreux, 33(2)

Favrieux (Seine-et-Oise), 85(1)
Ferté-Gaucher (la), (Seine-et-Oise), 98(1)
Foucaucourt (Somme), 106 (C)
Franciade (Saint-Denis), 14(2)
Fribourg-en-Brisgau, 61(2)

Gentilly, 80
Ghent, 80
Gothenburg, 123
Granville, 112 (H)
Grenelle, 45(1), 55, 87, 89(1), 90

Havre (le), 5, 81, 82

Javel, 100
Juliers, 60(1)

Laval, 60(2)
Liége, 26, 27, 51, 90(1), 123
Lille, 51, 80
London, 10, 61(3), 82
Lunéville, 15(3)
Lyon, 47(2), 90, 111

Maastricht, 80
Marles-en-Brie, 12
Marseille, 87
Meaux, 111 (N)
Metz, 98(1)
Meudon, 53, 54(1), 80
Méximieux, 19(4)
Mirepoix, 129
Mons, 61(3), 128
Montreuil-sous-Bois, 17(1)
Montrouge, 9(1), 12, 57, 80
Moray (Haute-Marne), 127
Morliac (Cantal), 106 (C)

Navarre (Seine-Inférieure), 106 (C)
Neaulbriez, 65(1)
Neuilly, 48, 66(1)

Odense, 61(1)
Olivet (Loiret), 20(2)
Orgères, 52

Paris: *bains* Poitevin, 5(2), 31(1);
bains Vigier, 37(2); *barrière* de
Belleville, 100(2); *barrière* de
Fontainebleau, 64; *barrière* du
Port-de-l'Eau, 45(1); Batignolles
(les), 45(1); Bicêtre, 12, 13(1),
19(3), 20, 20(3), 64, 65, 67, 76, 77,
79, 92; Bois de Boulogne, 43, 44,
45(1), 128; Champs-Elysées (les),
44, 45, 53, 54, 91, 128; *Divisions*:
Amis de la Patrie (des), 112 (H);
Arcis (des), 6, 37(1), 98(1);

Arsenal (de l'), 20(2), 98(1);
Bonconseil (du), 112 (H); Bondy
(de), 100(2); Bonne-Nouvelle
(de), 85, 88, 89; Brutus (de), 44(1),
107; Butte-des-Moulins (de la),
6, 10(1), 61(3), 96; Champs-
Elysées (des), 105; Cité (de la),
21(1), 38(1), 43, 128; Contrat-
Social (du), 113(1), 115 (K);
Fidélité (de la), 54(2); Finistère
(du), 3, 57; Fontaine-de-Grenelle,
(de la), 31(1), 61(3), 64(2), 107,
108, 109; Gardes-françaises (des),
20(3); Gravilliers (des), 48, 57,
116 (L); Halle-au-Bled (de la),
15(3), 114, 118; Halles (des), 46(2),
127; Indivisibilité (de l'), 57;
Invalides (des), 65(1), 88; Jardin
des Plantes (du), 75(1); Lombards
(des), 114; Marchés (des), 33(1),
57; Muséum (du), 4, 5(2), 6,
10(2), 12, 18, 32, 45(1), 55(2), 56,
63(1), 96, 127, 128, 129; Nord
(du), 11, 43, 57, 74(2), 78(2);
Ouest (de l'), 19(4), 66(1), 74(2),
106 (C); Panthéon-français (du),
6, 14(1); Poissonnière (du faubourg), 85; Popincourt (de), 6,
106 (C), 110 (F); Pont-neuf (du),
118; Réunion (de la), 61(2);
Temple (du), 48; Théâtre-français
(du), 106 (C); Thermes (des),
75(1); Tuileries (des), 37(2), 107,
110, 117, 118, 119; Unité (de l'),
75(1); Ecole Militaire, 87, 89;
escalier des Grands Degrés, 18;
Halle-aux-Vins (la), 124; Hotel-
Dieu (l'), 110, 111; *île* de la
Cité, 4, 106 (C); *île* des Cygnes,
48; *île* de la Fraternité, 106 (C);
île Louviers, 67(1); Incurables
(les), 65; Invalides (les), 67, 76;
jardin du Luxembourg, 44, 68(1);
jardin du Roi, 44(2); *Moulin-joli*
(au), 48, 99; Notre-Dame, 7, 43,

Paris – *contd.*

45; *Nouvelle-France* (*la*), 53;
Palais-Royal (le), 66, 80, 96;
parc Monceau (le), 45(1); Petites-
Maisons (les), 19(3), 67, 76, 77,
79; *Point-du-Jour* (*au*), 48, 99;
pompe Notre-Dame (la), 107 (D);
pont d' Asnières, 4; Pont-au-
Change, 49(1); *pont* de Charen-
ton, 4; *pont* de la Concorde, 52;
pont de Grammont, 67; Pont-
Neuf, 5(2), 15, 49(2), 74(1); *pont*
Royal, 15, 109, 110; *pont* de
Sèvres, 64(2); *pont* de Saint-
Cloud, 106 (C); *pont* de la
Tournelle, 25(3); *port* de l' Ecole,
15; de la Grenouillière, 31; de la
Mégisserie, 15; Nicolas, 18(2);
porte Saint-Antoine, 107 (D);
Saint-Bernard, 25(3); Saint-Denis,
64(1); *quais*: Dessaix, 49(1); de
l'Ecole, 15(3), 74(2); de la
Ferraille, 45(3); de Gêvres, 38(1),
45(3); Malaquais, 118 (N); de la
Mégisserie, 48, 105; de la Monnaie, 128; des Orfèvres, 61(1);
d'Orsay, 15; de la Rapée, 17(1);
de la Vallée, 14(1); Voltaire,
60(2); *rues, places, boulevards*, etc.;
Angervilliers (d'), 126; Antoine,
126; Arbre-Sec (de l'), 20(3), 86,
126, 127; Arcis (des), 118(O);
Bacq (du), 60(2); Ballets (des),
126; Barres (des), 126; Beaubourg,
61(2); Beaune (de), 31(1), 109;
Bercy (de), 75(1); Bertin-Poirée,
127; Bons-Enfants (des), 10(1);
Bordet, 49(1); Bouloy (du), 118
(O); Bourg-l'Abbé (du), 106 (C),
126; Cambrai (place), 14(1);
Capucines (boulevard des), 129;
Carrousel (place du), 111; Caumartin, 83(1); Chabanais, 128;
Chaise (de la), 19(4); Champ-
fleury, 128; Chantre (du), 126;

Chanvrerie (de la), 19(4); Chartrière, 14(1); Cherche-Midi (du),
17(2); Clichy (de), 75(1); Clos-
Denis (du), 85(1); Clos-Georges
(du), 60(1); Contrat-Social (du),
31, 126; Contrescarpe (de la),
20(2); Coquillière, 13(2), 126;
Cordiers (des), 126; Croix-des-
Petits-Champs, 19(3); Crucifix
(du), 19(4); Deux-Ecus (des),
116(2); Deux-Portes-Sauveur
(des), 112 (H); Enfer-Michel
(d'), 106 (C); Ferronnerie (de la),
57, 127; Fontaines (des), 116 (L);
Fossés-Marcel (des), 3(1); Fossés-
Saint-Germain (des), 127; Four-
Saint-Germain (du), 75(1); Four-
Saint-Honoré (du), 116 (K);
Fourreurs (des), 114 (J); Friperie
(de la Grande), 77(1); Froidmanteau, 13(2), 117 (M), 126;
Gaillon, 126; Germain-l'Auxerrois, 61(2); Gervais-Lanseul, 21
(1), 126; Grande-Truanderie (de
la), 19(3); Grenelle (de), 10(2);
Grenelle-Saint-Honoré (de), 114;
Grésillons (des), 113(I); Grève
(place de), 51, 52, 54; Helvétius,
60(1), 127; Honoré, 20(4), 61(2),
99; Hôtel-de-Ville (de l'), 86;
Huchette (de la), 75(1); Innocents
(charnier des), 100(2), 127; Innocents (place des), 33(1); Jardins
(des), 75(1); Jussienne (de la), 43,
128; Lappe (de), 86; Lille (de),
56, 61(3), 108; Lingerie (de la),
118 (N); Loi (de la), 97; Lombards (des), 86, 117; Lune (de la),
86, 88; Malte (de), 48(1); Marché-
d'Aguesseau (du), 126; Marchés
(des), 19(2); Martin (du faubourg), 43, 57, 75(2), 127; Mauvais-Garçons (des), 86, 91; Ménétriers (des), 61(2); Monnaie (de
la), 49(1); Montmartre (boule-

vard), 129; Montorgueil, 106 (C), 112 (H); Morfondus (des), 37; Mortellerie (de la), 37, 52, 53, 56, 86; Moulin (du Haut-), 38(1); Neuve-l'Egalité, 88; Nevers (de), 128; Nicaise, 18, 55(2), 90, 116 (L); Oratoire (de l'), 107 (C); Orléans (d'), 45(1); Oursine (de l'), 57; Pavée, 141; Petit-Carreau (du), 88, 108 (E); Petit-Musc (du), 37, 52, 53, 56, 113(1); Petit-Pont (du), 74(1); Petits-Champs (des), 128; Phélippeaux, 116 (L); Pirouette, 126; Plumet, 106 (C); Popincourt, 106 (C); Poulies (des), 60(1), 113 (J), 126; Pré (du), 17(1); Prêtres (des), 5; Prouvaires (des), 51(1); Quincampoix, 126; Réunion (de la), 57; Rousseau (Jean-Jacques), 55(1), 111(I), 126; Seine (de), 12; Sèvres (de), 5(2), 66(1), 100(1); Simon-le-Franc, 86; Sonnerie (de la), 63(1); Sorbonne (de la), 40(2); Saint-André-des-Arts, 16 (1); Saint-Antoine, 65(1), 98(1); Saint-Denis, 43, 47, 128; Saint-Denis (du faubourg), 117 (N); Saint-Dominique, 9(1), 126; Saint-Germain, 126; Saint-Germain-l'Auxerrois, 126, 128; Saint-Germain-l'Auxerrois (du Cloître), 128; Saint-Guillaume, 109; Saint-Honoré (du Cloître), 17(3); Saint-Honoré (du faubourg), 119; Saint-Honoré, 126; Saint-Jacques, 48; Saint-Marc, 55(1); Saint-Martin, 48; Saint-Nicolas, 86; Saints-Pères (des), 65(1), 108; Tannerie (de la), 98(1); Temple (boulevard du), 25(1); Temple (du), 116 (L); Thérèse, 107 (C); Tonnellerie (de la), 64(2); Tranquillité (de la), 76(1); Traversière-Honoré, 61(3), 126, 128;

Truanderie (de la), 33(1); Université (de l'), 60(2), 108; Vaugirard (de), 89; Verrerie (de la), 86; Vertbois (du), 126; Vertus (des), 57; Viarmes (de), 13(2), 15(3), 126; Victoires Nationales (des), 15(2), 128; Vieille-Tuerie (de la), 37; Vieilles-Etuves (des), 21(2), 56; Vieux-Augustins (des), 110; Vieux-Colombier (du), 85(1), 113(I); Villedot, 107 (C); Vivienne, 76(1); Saint-Eustache, 3(1)

Passy, 48, 51, 110(2)
Péronne, 80
Philadelphia, 14, 60(2), 124
Pollet (le) (Dieppe), 81, 82(1)
Pont-à-Mousson, 109
Pré-Saint-Gervais (le), 44(2)

Reims, 128
Rocroy, 59, 60(1), 127
Rouen, 55, 76(1), 82
Rusavoine (Oise), 5(3)

Sceaux, 11
Sèvres, 12, 15, 17(2), 80
Soisy-sous-Etiolle (Seine-et-Oise), 49(3)
Soëme-la-Grange (Meuse), 15(2)
Saint-Front (Orne), 57
Saint-Gargon (Doubs), 9(2)
Saint-Germain-en-Laye, 61(3), 85, 128
Saint-Martin-de-Bazoches (Seine-et-Oise), 110
Saint-Nicolas-de-Vérost (Mont-Blanc), 45(1)
Saint-Ouen, 12, 80

Valenciennes, 51, 80
Vaugirard, 12, 89

Venizy (Yonne), 21(1)
Versailles, 75(1), 110
Villeneuve-Saint-Georges, 111 (F)
Villejuif, 83(1)
Vimoutiers (Orne), 98(2)

Vitry-sur-Seine, 106 (C)

Wags (?) (Brabant), 123

Ybach, 61(2)